What Middle-Aged Men Want From Women

BY C. BRUCE WELLS

Cover Design & Photography by:

Charlene B. Stifter

Keith Trammel Photographic
www.TrammelPhoto.com

Barry W. Alt
www.a2zeds.com

© Copyright 2006 C. Bruce Wells
All rights reserved. No part of this publication may be reproduced, stored in a retrieval system, or transmitted, in any form or by any means, electronic, mechanical, photocopying, recording, or otherwise, without the written prior permission of the author.

Note for Librarians: A cataloguing record for this book is available from Library and Archives Canada at www.collectionscanada.ca/amicus/index-e.html
ISBN 1-4120-5029-4

Printed in Victoria, BC, Canada. Printed on paper with minimum 30% recycled fibre. Trafford's print shop runs on "green energy" from solar, wind and other environmentally-friendly power sources.

TRAFFORD
PUBLISHING

Offices in Canada, USA, Ireland and UK

Book sales for North America and international:
Trafford Publishing, 6E–2333 Government St.,
Victoria, BC V8T 4P4 CANADA
phone 250 383 6864 (toll-free 1 888 232 4444)
fax 250 383 6804; email to orders@trafford.com
Book sales in Europe:
Trafford Publishing (UK) Limited, 9 Park End Street, 2nd Floor
Oxford, UK OX1 1HH UNITED KINGDOM
phone +44 (0)1865 722 113 (local rate 0845 230 9601)
facsimile +44 (0)1865 722 868; info.uk@trafford.com
Order online at:
trafford.com/04-2838

10 9 8 7 6 5 4 3 2

To Char

Whose love, warmth, support, and bubbly personality made this book and my happiness possible. It was our destiny.

Contents

	Introduction	7
1	"Why Can't He Make A Commitment? What's Wrong With Him?"	11
2	What's The Worst Thing You Could Say To A Man?	20
3	What's The Best Thing You Could Say To A Man?	26
4	Can't He Think About Anything But Sex?	29
5	Don't Gossip About Our Secrets	39
6	How To Communicate With Your Man So He Understands	43
7	Men's Biggest Fears And Why You Should Know What They Are	56
8	What Men Like About Women Today	59
9	What Men Dislike About Women Today	62
10	"Swell. He's Having His Mid-Life Crisis! What Now?	66
11	Computer Dating And Other Places To Meet "Mr. Right"	70
12	"I Know That I Can Change Him"	82
13	How A Man Shows His Love For You	86
14	Feminism And Relationships. A Male Perspective	89
15	What Divorce Does To Middle-Aged Men	97

16	Why Men Hate Shopping, Coupons, And Self-Service	101
17	Why A Man's Job Comes Before You	108
18	Why Middle-Aged Men Have Affairs –"What Was He Thinking?"	111
19	Don't Keep Score Unless It's Football	118
20	What Kind Of Perfume Do Men Prefer?	120
21	What Is The Sexiest Thing A Woman Could Wear?	122
22	Why Bigger Is Always Better	124
23	"Honey, Just Leave Me Alone"	127
24	How To Compete With The Younger Woman And Win!	129
25	"I'm Always In A No-Win Situation"	135
26	"He Just Doesn't Care About Anything"	138
27	Men Need Respect	142
28	Men Need To Be Needed	145
29	Men Are Visual	147
30	"Stop The Constant Nagging"	149
31	"Why Ask For Directions? I'm Not Lost"	153
32	The Ideal Middle-Aged Woman	156
33	What Men Want To Tell Women In America Today	164
34	What Middle-Aged Men Want From Women	167

Introduction

What **do** middle-aged men really want from women today?

Men are very simple creatures (really) and don't require very much. Most men are low-maintenance. Women tend to make things more complicated than they need to be when dealing with men.

In many ways, men are dumb, naive, self-centered, and easily manipulated by women. We all know this from our past experiences.

You can get anything you want from a man if you approach and communicate with him in the right way. Unfortunately, most women want to do it the "woman's way." It doesn't work with men so women end up lonely, angry, and frustrated. It doesn't have to be that way!

According to the U.S. Bureau of the Census, there will be over 3 million women between the ages of 55 and 64 living alone in the year 2010. There will be 2.4 million men that age living alone too.

Since 1950, the number of divorced men has increased by 8 times while the total number of men has only doubled.

Women in their 40's have only a 32% chance of re-marrying

and women over age 50 have only a 12% chance.[1]

In 1920, there were 104 males for every female. In 1980, the number of males and females was about the same.

In other words, pickings are slim, ladies.

If you are married, you want to hold onto your man and your marriage but need the right tools.

If you are a single, divorced, or widowed middle-aged woman, your chances of re-marriage are remote indeed so you need to be able to relate to and attract "Mr. Right" or someone else will quickly snatch him up.

If he has had a full-time job for more than a week, is reasonably handsome, has a few strands of hair not used for a comb-over, has front teeth, and isn't gay or an ex-con, he is in big demand.

It is obvious that we have a problem and if this continues, we will all be living alone! Who really wants to live alone? It's depressing and no fun at all.

Warning: this book is **not politically correct**. It is written for the middle-aged woman (men don't read self-help books) who would like a little more insight into the workings of today's middle-aged men without the psycho-talk or sugar coating.

This book is not about how men should be or how you wish them to be; it's about how men really are. It comes from research, interviews, my own life experiences, and my totally unscientific survey of middle-aged men throughout the United States who really added spice to the book with their candor, humor, and surprisingly softer side.

[1] What Women Want–What Men Want by John Townsend. Oxford University.

Of course, not all men fit into the generalities I discuss in this book (Your man is probably a perfect communicator who anticipates and satisfies your every need) but there are common threads woven in most men you will find interesting and useful.

Throughout the book you will be thinking: "But what about **my** needs and wants? Don't **I** count for anything?" That will be in my next book (**"What Middle-Aged *Women* Want From Men"**) you can give to your man for Christmas, his birthday, or just when you are fed-up with him. Go to my website, www.cbrucewells.com and give me your thoughts in the survey so I can include them in the next book. It will be your way of telling men in America what **you** want from them!

This book is for a woman who wants to have a strong, long-term, committed relationship with a man. A man who is so much in love with you that he would willingly give his very life for you. A man who will adore and cherish you for the unique and special woman you are.

After reading this book, you will be better able to understand why men are the way they are, their idiosyncracies, and how to anticipate their actions. You will also be able to create environments conducive to your desires and dreams so you will be happier and more fulfilled.

So relax, curl up on a warm, comfortable sofa with lots of fluffy pillows and a cup of coffee as I take you on a little journey into the fascinating world of middle-aged men.

1

"Why Can't He Make A Commitment? What's Wrong With Him?"

*"O*nce you're committed, say goodbye to half your house and 90% of your sex life."[2]

That is how men feel about committing to a woman. They would rather face a hungry, mean bear in the woods than a woman looking for a commitment.

So how will you get him to commit to you?

Men are afraid to death of women. Seriously. Getting a man to make a commitment to a woman is the achievement of a woman's lifetime goal; for a man, it is the relinquishment of his (independence) and seen by some men as a miserable failure.

Women think men have this aversion to all commitments. It is one of the biggest complaints and frustrations women have with men and that is why I made this the first chapter of my book.

"Why can't this man make a commitment to our

---

[2] Why Men Don't Have a Clue and Why Women Always Need More Shoes by Barbara and Allan Pease. Broadway Books

relationship? How long will it take him? What's he waiting for?" It drives women insane because they can't settle for anything less than immediate, 100% total commitment by their men. Anything less than that is a personal affront to a woman. She is a failure in love. **"He hasn't proposed and we have been dating for 6 months. He must not really love me!"**

The fact is, a man does commit to those things and those people whom he wants to commit. He will commit his full energy to his job. He will commit his very life when he joins the military. He will commit his full resources to his children and protect them with his entire being. Men are not afraid to commit. They readily make commitments every day in their jobs. They are hesitant to commit to a woman because of the vast emotional and financial responsibilities and obligations imposed upon them with this commitment. They know the burden and long-term responsibilities which come with this commitment and they don't take it lightly.

Men have also learned the punishment they will receive if the relationship does not succeed. From the woman, from the courts, from their friends, and from their own families. He will be blamed as the one who could not make the relationship work. It must be his fault.

Men purposely take their time before making an emotional commitment. Sometimes a very, very, very long time. Sometimes never.

The feminist movement made it easier for men **not** to commit. In the late 60's, birth control for women became common and gave women more control over sex without the responsibility of pregnancy. Sex became more casual. A woman used to keep men at bay with: "I can't. I might get pregnant." Not anymore. Along with this "free sex" attitude came the realization to men that they no longer had to commit (or say they would) in order to have intimacy with a woman.

Women thought the sexual revolution elevated their position. In reality, it brought them down a notch in men's eyes.

Today, middle-aged men have a readily available pool of women willing to share sex with them at any time, anywhere. They don't have to commit in order to have sex anymore. This has made it even more difficult for a woman to get a man to commit. Why buy the cow if he can get the milk for free?

A woman today has to offer much more than sex in order to get a man to commit. Long gone are the days when a woman could lure a man into a commitment with the promise of blissful and perpetual sexual favors. She had better also have the personality, intelligence, and charisma to attract and keep the man. A woman today has a heavy burden of convincing a man that she is "worthy" of commitment.

"Men fall in love because of the way they feel about themselves when they are with you."[3]

Make sure he feels comfortable and loved when he is with you; not anxious about your next criticism, put-down, or expectation. Compliment him and make him feel like the most important person in your life. He should feel like the greatest man in the world when he is with you.

He will commit himself to a woman when he feels that she is the best one for him and there is no one better out there. There is this fear in men that if they commit to one woman, there may be someone more "perfect" right around the corner waiting for them. Someone with a better personality, who likes to do more things with him, is more attuned to his likes and dislikes,

[3] Light His Fire by Ellen Kreidman. Villard Books

someone with thinner thighs or is better in bed and satisfies him more.

Continually reinforce to him that you are the perfect woman for him in every way and no one could ever be better for him than you. The two of you are perfect together!

He may not commit to you simply because you are not "the one" he has been looking for and he is afraid to tell you and hurt your feelings. It's not that he can't commit; he may just not want to commit to **you**.

Don't say: **"What's your problem? Why can't you get off your duff and make some decisions about our future together? I want to know where we stand and I want to know now! I'm not getting any younger, you know!"** You need to be kind and gentle (not demanding and hostile) to elicit his true feelings so you can find out if you need to move on and let him (and you) keep searching. He will tell you the truth if he doesn't feel threatened and thinks you can handle the news without yelling and blaming him.

Keep in mind that men are afraid of women because they know that women have the emotional upper-hand. Women are very intimidating to men. Men are very strong in many other areas but not in relationship or emotional matters. They are weaklings and they know it. You know it too. Right?

Men need to be independent and in control. Emotional commitment is a threat to a man's independence and he has to give up some control in order to commit to a relationship. Men don't like to be in weak positions. They feel vulnerable and very uncomfortable. If the woman comes across as too strong and demanding, the man will back away as he realizes that he will lose too much independence and control in the relationship and that is unacceptable to him no matter how appealing the woman is to him in other respects.

Most first marriages end in divorce and even more second marriages fail. We all know the odds are against us. Is it any wonder middle-aged men don't want to commit a second time? It could be a second big mistake and men hate to be failures at anything let alone multiple failures. It is better not to commit and take the heat from you rather than face another failure. He has to feel totally confident this new relationship will last. If he doesn't, it's not worth the risk of making a commitment.

He will need to know about your financial condition before becoming serious so be prepared to share everything with him. No surprises later that you have a zillion dollars on credit cards that he has to pay off. He needs to know what he's getting into. There can be no fear of the unknown. He is afraid enough about other things. If he doesn't share his finances with you too, beware. He may be hiding things or just doesn't trust you. Not a healthy situation when you are building a foundation for commitment.

Men commit for intimacy and love. Odds are that they won't get those. Men have learned that once a woman has hooked them and get the security they desire, sex and intimacy are soon forgotten or ignored. Men feel betrayed and humiliated and don't want to be in that position again. Read the chapter: "Can't He Think About Anything But Sex?"

"Five times as many women as men have no desire to make love."[4] No desire to make love? Did the man agree to that when he got married? Did you tell him that you would "be in the mood" only a couple of times a month after you get married? No! It's no wonder divorces, affairs, and lack of commitment by men are on the rise. It is the ultimate deception and betrayal not to have sex with the man you expect to be loyal and provide you security

---

4   The Act of Marriage After Age 40 by Tim & Beverly Lahaye. Zondervan Pub.House

and then blame him when he does not uphold his commitments to you. You were not consistent with your commitments either.

Did you ever watch that television program "The Bachelor?" It is about a bunch of desperate young women trying their best to snare this one pathetic-looking guy. They are eliminated one-by-one until he chooses one "lucky" woman. It is a silly and, in my opinion, a women-degrading program. All of these young women blindly chasing this guy for some kind of prize at the end pretending he is the man of their dreams. But when you hear what the women are really saying behind the guy's back, it shows how devious and two-faced women become when they are trying to win a man. They will do and say anything to get him committed. You know that they are not the person they portray themselves to be to the dumb bachelor. You don't understand why he picked the back-stabber over the princess because you know what she was saying behind his back.

Men are relationship morons. They can't see through a woman's smoke screen. They are emotionally blind. Other women can see through the screen immediately and don't understand why the bachelor is so "stupid." It's no wonder men have a hard time committing when they are so often and so easily deceived. They know that they can be easily duped with promises of affection, fake interest in football games, and the promise of candle-lit meals every night so are leery of making commitments.

Of course, men can easily see through other men and wonder why women are so naive not to see what is going on there too. Men understand men. Women understand women. We just don't have a clue about each other!

It is bewildering to men when they see a beautiful, intelligent, personable woman with some long-haired, tattooed, skinny, drug-infested, freak of a guy. We think: "What is she doing with that guy when she could have anyone she wants?" She probably thinks she can change him. She is a "converter." Or maybe she has such a low opinion of herself that she has to settle for the creep. It confuses men.

Relationships with women have been compared to buying a car. When you drive off the lot with that new car it is exhilarating. You feel like a million bucks! You think that feeling will last forever. After 20,000 miles, it is just a way to get around. After 50,000 miles, the new smell is gone and you realize what you bought requires high maintenance, is hard to start when cold, unpredictable, and unreliable. Don't become that old car.

If you want a man to commit to you, he must trust you first. Men are afraid of women because women have always held the emotional upper-hand and men know it. He must trust that you will give him the intimacy he desires without conditions, ultimatums, or threats and that you will not change after he commits to you. He has to feel comfortable with you; not on edge wondering what you will demand from him next or how he has failed you once again. He has to trust that you will not hurt him.

He will test you in little ways to see if you are for real or are just pretending to be that nice, charming, sexy woman who will then turn into a nag and make his life miserable.

He may want sex from you two nights in a row just to see if you show an interest even though he's not sure himself if he can "get in the mood" again right away. Or he may say that he doesn't want to visit your sister and her dead-beat husband this weekend so he can stay home and watch the big game on television and wait to see your reaction.

When he sees that you are really the woman you appear to be, he will open more of his heart to you and will want to please you in all the ways you want. He won't keep testing you after he sees that your actions are true to your words.

Don't pressure him to commit. He will either do it on his own or he will not. And he will do it in his own time; not yours.

If you pressure him too much to make fast commitments, he will just back away and you have accomplished nothing or he will give you a false commitment just to appease you. Be warm and supportive so he trusts his heart to you.

He will let you know when he is ready to commit himself to you and it will be real and genuine. Why would you want someone who only commits to you because you talked him into it? Don't settle for a forced commitment just because you're impatient. It's not worth anything and it won't last.

If he doesn't commit to you in the period of time you think reasonable, you may have to end the relationship and look for someone new. He may never commit to you.

What is a reasonable amount of time before expecting a total commitment? For a man, it is probably twice what a woman thinks is reasonable. If you think one year is fair, make it two years for the man. If you think 3 months, get a reality check. You are acting desperate and desperate is not appealing.

You must also look at what he has been through. If he just came out of a divorce or long-term relationship, you know it will take him a long time to make another total commitment because he is gun-shy. Be patient. He will bounce back in his own time and it will be sooner if you are kind, gentle, and not demanding.

Live for today. Obsessing about commitments without enjoying what you have today is a waste of precious time. There is nothing wrong with enjoying the moment. You might not be around tomorrow. Sometimes the journey is as enjoyable as reaching the destination.

Enjoy each other's company. Relish the happy times you go to that little bed-and-breakfast in the mountains, walk the trail through the woods listening to the singing birds and babbling brooks, or just sitting on the porch in your backyard with a cup of coffee reading the Sunday newspaper discussing current events together.

Be patient with your man.

The commitments will come when it is the right time for both of you so free yourself to enjoy life and be happy with what you have rather than worrying about what you don't have. He will come around when he is ready and trusts you with his heart.

2

What's The Worst Thing You Could Say To A Man?

Men are very sensitive to what you say.

I know, it's hard to imagine your man is ever really listening to you while the television is on let alone being sensitive about what you say! But when he is listening, he takes what you say literally and at face value. He will not read into what you say to find hidden meanings. You need to know how men will react to what you say and stay away from certain topics.

Here are some quotes taken from my survey of middle-aged men which you should **never say to a man.** These are words which are the most hurtful to a man and can never be taken back after you say them.

"I don't need you anymore." Men need to be needed by their women so this can be devastating to a man.

"I don't trust you."

"You call that a penis?" As you know, men are very self-conscious about size. Size matters.

"You need to change for me." Men don't change and won't change even for you. What you see is what you get in a man.

"That's it?" You can take that anyway you want!

"You bore me to tears." All men think they are the most exciting thing that ever happened to women so they can't stand anyone thinking they are boring.

"Honey, I'm in love with someone else."

"I'm leaving you for another woman." Being in love with another man is bad enough, but leaving for another woman is really bad. It's the ultimate insult to his manliness.

"I regret ever marrying you." He trusted you enough to commit and marry you. This negates everything he did for you and he will be devastated.

"I don't respect you anymore." Respect is one of the most important things to a man so when you take that away, he will feel worthless.

"We need to talk." This is one of the most feared statements to a man.

"You're stupid." He knows that already so don't rub it in.

"I hate you." He will take that literally and not that you hate some of the things he does.

"That wasn't funny."

"I'm pregnant." That's probably not so important when dating after menopause.

"Is it in yet?" Refer back to: "You call that a penis?"

"You are a failure at your job." It is critical for a man to know that you are proud of his job and that he can support his family.

Keep in mind that if you criticize or belittle a man's means of living, manhood, pride, or self-worth, he will retaliate by becoming angry, resentful, reclusive, and absent.

Choose your words carefully, remembering that he will take what you say literally as men can't interpret hidden meanings and you won't be able to take-back what you said later as the damage will have been done.

You may think what you said is a reflection on your inner feelings and not just that one situation.

You are frustrated that he hasn't asked for a raise because the family's finances are in a shambles so you tell him his job is worthless. He interprets that to mean that what he has been doing for years to support his family has been worthless and he is worthless too; not that you are trying to encourage him to do better and make more money for the family. He can't read into what you are saying. He only takes the literal meaning.

Read the chapter on communication so you better know how a man interprets your words and use the above quotes at your own peril.

Want to end your new relationship with a man very quickly? Just say: **"Where Do We Stand?"**

After just a couple of dates, women just can't resist asking this question as it eats at them right from the beginning of the relationship. You are asking a man to make a commitment and to make the relationship permanent. He is not ready for that kind of talk.

He will let you know that he is ready when he starts talking about long-range plans with you.

Don't be pushy. Men don't like pushy women. It takes a long time for a man to process anything emotional and you need to be patient. Of course, if you have been dating a man for 5 years and there is no talk of marriage or commitment, he is probably not really interested in you and you should move on and stop wasting time on him.

Never criticize his job, his mother, his kids from a previous marriage, his car, his loss of hair, his lovemaking, the size of his penis, his past, his driving, or that he can't find his car in the parking garage.

Don't tell him on the first date that you have been in therapy for the past 50 years and how much it has helped you deal with life, your failed marriage, and your gay sister. He will think you are a wacko even though you think you are sharing something very special and intimate about yourself with him.

The same thing goes with astrology and how compatible your signs are. He doesn't care that you are a Leo who likes to make stuffed bunnies and pink nose warmers and thinks it strange for anyone to bring that up when he's just trying to get to know you.

A middle-aged woman told me: **"I think most middle-aged men go for the teeny-boppers and can't handle a real woman their own age."** We can handle the women our age but choose not to because many of them are so nasty. Talking negatively about men in general will lead him to think you are one of those men-hating women and he won't call you again. Men don't like mean women. Talk nice. Save your criticisms for later or just forget about them entirely.

Never correct a man in front of others. **Never**. It is a direct affront to his manhood and he will not tolerate it for long. It makes no difference who is right or what the situation is. Talk to him later in private if you have a beef with him but never do it in front of others no matter how minor the concern.

If he takes you out to eat, don't complain about your food, the restaurant, or the service. Not only is it rude to insult your host, he will feel like he has failed you.

Never complain to the waiter. Tell your man and he will decide whether or not it is worth taking on the waiter. Leave it up to him. When you go around your man and voice your displeasure to the waiter, your man will feel like he is not good enough for you and you have no respect for him. He is embarrassed in front of another person and he will be upset at you no matter what the original problem was. If he doesn't want to complain to the waiter and you do, just drop it. He made the decision. Be gracious and let it go.

"Wesley, we have been exclusive for 8 months, two days, and 4 hours. I have decided it is time for us to set a date to get married. If you don't set the date right now, I will have to look for someone else as I'm not getting any younger, you know." He tells you not to let the door hit you in the butt on the way out.

Never give a man an ultimatum unless you are prepared for the worst outcome as men will not relent on any ultimatums. You may think you are just giving him a little pressure to do what you want him to but then find out he does just the opposite and will not turn back or compromise later. It is a challenge to his masculinity and he cannot back down. Ultimatums are very dangerous when used with men so tread lightly.

Make your man feel appreciated, loved, and respected. Be

aware of what you say to him knowing that he will interpret what you say at face value and you won't be able to take it back or talk your way out of it later.

3

What's The Best Thing You Could Say To A Man?

We saw in the last chapter what **not** to say to a man. Now we can look at those things men most like to hear from women.

"I love you." That is the most frequent phrase mentioned by men that they yearn to hear from you. I know, you want to hear "I love you" from him too, but he won't do that on his own so you will have to prod him a little (and buy my next book "What Middle-Aged Women Want From Men" so you can give it to him for Christmas or your anniversary).

"I totally dig the whole package." Men love to hear how "buff" they look even if they look 8 months pregnant and have to do a "comb-over" because they lost most of their hair. Make him think he could be a center-fold in "Playgirl" magazine! In his mind, he is a "hotty" so don't destroy that illusion! Build him up!

"Your wife sure is lucky." This was mentioned by only one man in the survey so don't get too concerned. It was probably just a joke. Probably...

"There's nothing I'd rather do than be with you." Wow! You will have the man in the palm of your hands with that!

"I like you."

"You were AWESOME." I assume this is when the man actually brought the right items home from the grocery store...

"I want you."

"You are an amazing lover." Amazing means I was good. Right?

"You're funny." Men love a woman with a sense of humor and those who appreciate a man's light-heartedness.

"You're a great person."

"I'm not pregnant." Read the chapter "How To Compete With The Younger Woman."

"Can we please have sex tonight in a new position?" The guy will probably think he is having a dream! It can't be reality!

"You are my best friend."

"Oh, you are so big!" Men think that if they have a big penis, they will better satisfy their women and are better lovers. Let him think whatever he wants.

"I'll be your best friend forever." I don't know why men want to hear "best friend" all the time but they do!

So there you have it ; all those things you should remember to say to a man to make him happy!

You can use all of these phrases repeatedly as men have a short attention span and tendency to easily forget things women say!

4

Can't He Think About Anything But Sex?

So why is it that men are obsessed with sex? Even middle-aged men want more sex!

"Don't they think of anything else but sex?"

"Don't they know a woman wants affection, cuddling, and lots of talk before she can be 'in the mood' for sex?"

"Can't he just love me for me without sex getting in the way?"

The simple answer is: no. He can't love you without the sexual connection. And he doesn't understand why all the pretense leading up to sex. **"Why can't she just have sex with me without all the fuss?"**

"How often do people think about sex? Men: on average, 203 times a day."[5]

A survey by Longevity Magazine indicated 70% of men would like to make love more than 3 times per week. Only 37% of women feel the same. We are definitely not on the same

---

[5] Women Who Stay With Men Who Stray by Debbie Then, Ph.D. –Hyperion

wave-length here folks.

I don't think middle-aged men think about sex 203 times per day. It's probably just about 150 or so. Just kidding! But men do think about having sexual relations a lot and are usually frustrated because the women they are with don't want to have sex as often as they. Women think they are having too much sex. Men think it's not enough.

So are men just stupid sex fiends or are there other reasons men need sex so much more than women?

I am going to tell you something extremely important that could change your relationship with your man forever. If you do not heed this, your relationship with your man will not be deep, endearing, or last the eternity you envision. **Having sex with your man is as important to him as communication is to you.**

Women value communication as extremely important in a relationship (**"We never talk!"**) but trivialize sex with their men as an "extra" thing to do; a chore or burden to be tolerated as the price for marriage and security.

Sex is how a man communicates his emotions and bonds with his mate. He has a difficult time communicating emotions with words and therefor does it through the act of sex. It is his way of talking with you and showing his closeness and vulnerability. It is the time he is most vulnerable and men hate to be vulnerable with anything so you know it is important to him.

He can't do it with words so he communicates with his actions. It's not just the act of sex. It is how he talks with you. Of course, he needs that physical release but he also needs that bond with his woman.

How would you feel if your man did not talk with you for a week or a month or a year? Not one word. If you said: "Great! I need the peace and quiet," you don't need this book!

Women need communication through words; they need to talk and talk and talk. They thrive on talk.

With men, only actions count. Not having sex with him is the same as you not having conversation with him. If he does not have sex with you at least a couple of times per week, he will withdraw, not do what you ask, and eventually leave you for someone who will (or promises she will) have sex with him all the time. It is that important to a man. It is that simple and direct.

I know, you think I'm full of it. Right? Most women brush the idea of sex as a man's way of communication aside by saying: "He just wants to get off to satisfy himself and then go about his own activities." Trivializing his need for sex to bond and communicate with you is one of the worst mistakes you could make. Go ahead and think you're right and joke about it with your girlfriends but you will be alone.

We all know that women use sex to manipulate men and it is a strong influence over men. To have this power and abuse it can lead to disaster in the relationship. Use that power wisely and don't underestimate the consequences.

"Tests show that a man who has a pent-up need for sex has difficulty hearing, thinking, driving, or operating heavy machinery."[6] You don't want your man having accidents with heavy machinery; do you? A man needs sex for his emotional and physiological well-being. It's not just lust.

---

6   Why Men Don't Listen and Women Can't Read Maps by Barbara and Allan Pease– Broadway Books

How many men divorce their wives because they have been getting too much sex at home? A man will not stay in love with a woman if he isn't getting sex or if the sex is no good (the woman just lays there and yawns while looking at her watch to see if she's missing an episode of "Sex and the City".)

I know; the politically correct thing to say would be: **"He should love me no matter what. Love shouldn't be contingent on having sex."** That is simply not true. Men don't think that way in spite of what they will tell you or how you think it should be in a perfect world. As you know, men are not politically correct!

He will lie to you and tell you that he will love you for eternity even if you only want lousy sex once per month. He will tell you that he understands you being tired all the time and having mysterious headaches because today's man is warm, caring, and feminized.

He doesn't want to appear weak by begging for sex or cause a big argument that he never wins anyway. He doesn't want to admit that he has been duped by his mate. But he will remember this when an attractive woman comes on to him and promises wild sex every hour for the rest of his life. It doesn't matter that she is lying to him. It doesn't matter that it will cost him a fortune in Viagra and divorce lawyers. She promises to give him what he needs and he will be vulnerable (stupid). Don't make him vulnerable by holding back sex from him.

"Once she gets the ring, I get no sex."

"Scientists have discovered a food that diminishes a woman's sex drive by 90%... wedding cake." [7]

"We were having sex almost every day before we got married.

---

7   Women Can't Hear What Men Don't Say by Warren Farrell Ph.D. Penguin Putnam Inc.

Now she says she is tired, has a headache, doesn't have time, or some other assache." She said: "I'd rather clean the toilet than have sex!" Men feel betrayed and angry.

Men are very simple-minded. They think that if they were having sex with a certain frequency and intenseness before marriage, it would stay the same. Why would she change? It would be like changing the rules of a football game during the game to favor one team. He would say that's not fair and stop the game. If you are having sex with your man three times per week in the beginning of the relationship, you better have that now or wind down before asking a man for a life-time commitment.

It's not fair to expect your man to be consistent providing security and the faithfulness you expected and not hold up your end of the bargain no matter what the excuses. Men don't care what the excuses for not having sex are. It is simply a rejection of them and men can't handle rejection in any form.

If you change how often you want sex with your man, don't get upset when he makes changes in the relationship too.

If you take your man for granted, he may not be there in the future for you as he sees not having sex with him as a betrayal and will not feel remorse in betraying you. Be open and consistent.

If you tell your man that you have a "head-ache" or you're "too tired" to have sex, he hears: "I don't love you anymore and I don't want you." "You're no longer desirable to me." He doesn't think rationally when it comes to sex.

Be a lady and a tramp.

Males want to have sex with as many women as possible as that is their physiological sex drive. They are not naturally monogamous. They want variety and if they don't get it from their woman, they will get it elsewhere.

Outside of the bedroom, men want a woman they can be proud of. She should look attractive, have a good sense of humor, smiles, and is clean, trim, intelligent, and respectable. Inside the bedroom, a man wants a sexual, immodest woman who is a little slutty.

Every time he has sex with you, he wants it to be a little different. Like being with a different woman each time. It is his fantasy.

It could be simply wearing a different sexy negligee or wearing your hair a different way. Or perhaps asking him to take a shower with you first and lather him down.

Have sex with him in different places and in different ways. Meet him one day at the door wearing his trench coat and nothing on underneath. Ask him to meet you at a motel like you were sneaking around with a sexy stud (in his mind he is one). The list is endless. Don't worry about being embarrassed. He may joke a little in the beginning because he's not used to this attention but he will love it!

Be ten different women to him so he is always challenged and he will be devoted to you forever because you are satisfying him.

Whatever you do, be sexy. Don't wear ugly flannel pajamas to bed, give up make-up or having your hair done professionally, wear a bra that is too small, or have bad breath or yellow teeth. He wants a real, sexy woman. Be all the women he dreams of!

I'm The Best You Ever Had. Right?

It is extremely important to always reinforce to your man that he is the best sex partner you have ever had. Ok, maybe he isn't. Maybe you would rather shampoo your rugs than have sex with him. But you picked him so he must be the best! Right?

Never, **never** compare him with another man. Men can't handle comparisons as they will feel you are not satisfied. Lie to him if you must. He is the best lover you have ever had or ever hope to have. Tell him that every time you make love to him. After a while, he will probably believe it.

Since men are so obsessed with how they perform in bed, never use his sexual prowess (or lack of it) in the heat of an argument. If you say: "You're an ass for not doing anything around the house, and I just fake orgasms because you don't turn me on," you will do irreparable harm to your relationship as he will never forget that and he will never trust you again. You will have satisfied your need to hurt him at the moment but the cost to you will be great.

There are some things you can never take back and telling a man he is inadequate in bed is one of them. His manhood is most important to him. You will live to regret criticizing a man about his sexual ability. He will consider the relationship with you to be worthless if he can't satisfy you sexually and he may not bounce back.

Don't Expect a Man to Talk to You During Sex

Did you ever try and talk with a man when he is watching television? What about when he is driving and trying to find an address? Or when he is having sex with you? He will tune you out because he can only concentrate on one thing at a time.

Women call men dumb because men only think about one thing at a time. Men have tunnel vision because instinctively, they had to concentrate as hunters in order to bring home a meal for their families. They focus on the kill. Women can think about their hair appointment, talk with their girlfriends on the phone, do their makeup, and do brain surgery all at the same time. That's because women can think with both sides of their brains at the same time so they process more information than a man.

Men are simple creatures. They have to think about just one thing and then go on to the next idea. They think with just one side of their brain as fibers between the two sides are thinner in men than in women and cannot process as much information. Obviously, this just confirms what women have been saying for years: **"Men only think about one thing."** Women just didn't realize that "one thing" is not necessarily sex.

When a man is having sexual intercourse with you, he cannot easily talk with you at the same time. It's not that he doesn't want to talk his heart out to you or that he doesn't want to communicate his feelings for you in this most intimate of times. His mind won't let him. He is on over-load (no pun intended!). You may think he is being insensitive or just wants to have sex without emotion or contact but that is not the case. His mind won't allow him to concentrate on the sex act and talk at the same time. That would be trying to do two things at once and we know men can't do that.

Remember, men can only do one thing at a time. Don't believe me? That's because you think as a woman and not a man. Let him enjoy the sexual experience by concentrating on just that and nothing else. Realize his limitations and not make it into something it's not. He doesn't understand why it takes you hours to warm up but goes along with that so how about putting up with his silence?

Since he can't talk with you during sex, don't ask a man questions or talk too much. You know what it's like when the dentist asks you questions at the same time he is working in your mouth? Feel helpless because you can't talk? It's the same way men feel when you talk with them during sex. "Do you love me honey?" "How does that feel to you?" "Did you get the oil changed in the car today?" He is thinking: "Shut up and just enjoy this fantastic feeling without the distractions of talk." If you must talk, tell him how big he is, how great a sex partner he is, or that you are totally satisfied with him. Don't ask him questions.

Never tell him what to do during sex, that he is doing something wrong, or what you read in the latest woman's magazine about how sex should be. He will think you are being pushy and not satisfied with what he is doing because all men think they are the best lovers in the world. He will feel rejected and shut down entirely.

Show him what pleases you. If you want him to touch you in a certain place, take his hand and put it there and show him that it pleases you. He wants to please you as much as he wants pleasure himself. As a matter-of-fact, many men take more pleasure in satisfying their mates than themselves.

Make sure he knows that you enjoy what he is doing but will enjoy it even more if he does certain other things. You can make him into a stud lover who will totally satisfy if you approach him in the right way so he thinks it is his idea, not your being disappointed that he was doing it "wrong" before.

For some reason, a man needs to see that his mate is brought to orgasm. It is a male "thing." If she doesn't have an orgasm (multiple orgasms are even better), he feels that he was a failure at sexually satisfying her and that makes him a total failure.

Keep in mind that men are goal and results orientated. A man must have an orgasm to be satisfied so he thinks that is the only way a woman will be satisfied too. You may find the act of sex pleasurable without climaxing but your man will think it is a waste of time and that he is a failure as a man and lover if you don't climax. Talking to him about how great it is for you even without an orgasm will not make any difference. No amount of talk will change his mind or make him feel better. Fake orgasms if you must. Scream with pleasure. Writhe in passion. But have an orgasm or he will lose interest in you.

A sexless relationship is no relationship at all for a man. He cannot fully love you without a good sex life.

Understand that sex is what will keep your man interested and vital so nourish that constantly and he will be there for you. It is how he communicates his love for you. Let him "talk" with you as often as possible!

5

Don't Gossip About Our Secrets

"Oh, Janine, I know you are just my nail girl but I just HAVE to tell you how mad I am at Don. He won't take me out every Friday night like he used to and he complains that we don't have enough sex even though I let him almost every month or so. He is being such a ninny. What do you think I should do?"

Women have this propensity to gossip about everything thinking it is just idle talk. They feel better after talking things out. They want answers and advice from others. They love gossiping and also love hearing gossip. Look at the popularity of the daytime talk shows and the reality television programs. It is all gossip. They can't get enough of it.

Men don't gossip because they only care about actions and results. Gossiping to men is an annoying waste of time because it rarely ends in a decision to do something. It is just talk. The exception to this is police officers. I was a cop. They gossip about everything and anything. They love to gossip and there is plenty to gossip about in police work. They are like a bunch of old ladies.

Ever see two police cars pulled up next to each other? Think they are talking about an important investigation? No way. They are just gossiping. "I've got to pull an extra shift this week because the ass-hole Sergeant wants to take time off with his new honey." Or "I had to arrest that dirt-bag John Smith again because he stole cans from a dumpster behind the grocery store yesterday. I hate the paperwork." Sometimes it is good because you hear about what people in your district are doing so when you come across them, you can handle the situation better. Most of the time, it is just idle gossip.

It may be that police see the most horrible things and this is a way to release that frustration and anxiety. The only people they can talk with about these things are other officers as civilians wouldn't understand or may try to use it against them. Police officers learn not to trust anyone or anything because when they do, it bites them in the butt. They also have to be calm and in control at all times when everything is out of control. The divorce and suicide rate of cops is twice the general population. It's probably because of all that gossiping!

Men are very closed-mouthed about their emotions and innermost feelings. They consider these revelations as top secret and cannot even imagine sharing this kind of information with anyone else. It would not even occur to them to talk with friends or relatives about anything emotional let alone strangers. If he shares something on an emotional level with you, it is a big thing to him and not just casual conversation like you have with your girlfriends every day. He is trusting his feelings and his vulnerability with you like you do when you agree to having sexual relations with a man.

Never (and I mean NEVER) talk to others about your sex life unless you are prepared to lose your man forever. Sex is one of the most important aspects of a man's feeling of self-worth and if you share that with someone else, he will think you are saying he is inadequate and useless. He will leave you. It might take some time but he will leave you because he no longer trusts you with his confidence. If he is great in bed and you just have to spill your guts to someone, go ahead, but realize he will still be embarrassed and there will be that lingering doubt in his mind that you are sharing other personal things he doesn't want anyone else to know.

If a man finds out later that you shared his emotional secrets with anyone (that means anyone-no exceptions) he will feel betrayed and humiliated. You may have a million excuses (**"I just told my sister and she won't tell anyone else. Really. It's not a big deal anyway so why are you over-reacting?"**) but it will be too late.

He is not "over-reacting." He is being a man and you need to understand and appreciate that. In his eyes, you can no longer be trusted and he will not confide his feelings with you in the future. You will be ostracized from his feelings for a long time and will have to earn his trust back. This seems trivial to a woman who shares everything with anyone who will listen and most women don't take this seriously until it is too late. Beware!

Never gossip about your man's failures. This is especially true about a man's job. After sexual adequacy, a man's job defines his self-worth and anything that diminishes his self-worth is extremely painful for a man. Men hate to fail at anything and when their women tell others about those failures, it is even more humiliating and there will be a back-lash. Keep his failures between the two of you.

He buys a new car and then finds out later that he paid $1,000 more than he should have. He reluctantly shares that humiliation with you. After all, men are supposed to be macho and able to negotiate the best deals when going through that tortuous haggling with the car dealer. Right? His wife then tells her neighbor girlfriend. They get a laugh because they think it wasn't very important and it gets back to him through the neighbor's husband. He is incensed that his wife shared that failure and is mad at her. He feels his trust has been violated. She doesn't understand why he is angry. It was just a little thing. She didn't think it was any big deal but all failures are a big deal to a man.

Sometimes repeated failures will lead a man to commit suicide. It is that important to a man to feel successful at everything. Don't take that away from him.

If you must gossip about us (I know, you just can't help yourself), then only gossip about our accomplishments and successes. Men love to hear that their women are proud of them because men are goal orientated and need to feel successful.

If you're not sure whether or not to talk to your friends about something personal he shared with you, just ask him. If he says he is not comfortable with you releasing that information to the world, respect his wishes.

Some women will go out and tell their friends confidential information even after he has asked them not to and that is total disregard for his feelings. He will be angry, resentful, and not trust you.

You want him to share his feelings with you. You want him to trust you. You want to be his best friend. Be careful what you say to others so you don't alienate your man. He will appreciate and love you more if he knows that what he shares with you won't be spread around.

6

How To Communicate With Your Man So He Understands

"He doesn't talk to me about how he really feels or about our relationship. I don't think he cares."

"He should understand how I feel and what I want without my having to tell him. After all, we've been together for 10 years!"

"I try to talk to him about how I feel and he just turns me off. He doesn't listen. What a jerk!"

"Men are insensitive and not in touch with their emotions. They should be more like women"

Ever catch yourself thinking or even saying those things? The simple fact is: men and women have a difficult time communicating with each other and it seems to be getting worse. We just don't think the same.

Outdoor Rafting Guide said: "As long as women get their information about men from other women, they will always get it wrong." It's just like trying to talk with someone who speaks another language you don't understand. It's very frustrating, you talk louder thinking that will help, and eventually you just give up trying to understand what they are saying.

Women complain about their men not communicating with them almost as much as they lament about men not making commitments.

Studies have shown that couples spend only about 30 minutes per week in real conversation. Only 30 minutes per week! That's less time than you talk with your hairdresser!

When was the last time you had a nice, meaningful conversation (not: "Who's going to pick up dinner tonight?") with your man?

Lack of communication between middle-aged men and women is one of the biggest causes of relationship breakdowns. It is extremely frustrating for both men and women. Yes, men too! We get frustrated because you don't understand us either!

First of all, men have a physiologically difficult time tapping into the part of their brain that handles feelings and emotions. Women can go right into that room but men have to climb over obstacles before they can open that door. Their brains are set up differently. The left side of our brains control factual and logic information. The right side controls communications, feelings, and emotions. The fibers connecting the left and right sides are 40% larger in women so they can process more information faster and easier than men.

Do you have a computer with internet? It is like connecting to the internet. Women have high-speed cable and men have that old, slow dial-up that idles when there is too much information coming in and regularly crashes.

Studies have shown that it takes men up to 7 hours longer than women to process emotional information. 7 hours! That's why you see the dumb look on his face when you talk about your feelings or ask him how he feels about your relationship. He is on overload!

Men can't move out of the left logical side to the emotional quickly or easily. It takes them time to get in and once they are in that emotional room, they want to get out as quickly as possible because it is uncomfortable and even a dangerous feeling to them.

Men are instinctive hunters and being in that emotional room makes them vulnerable to attack. They don't like to be closed in; especially emotionally. You can see that look on his face. Confusion, hostility, and fear. Like a caged animal. Right?

Men really don't want to talk and they think women talk too much. One response from my survey of men said: **"Sometimes talking just kills the perfect day."**

I know that comes as a shock to one or two of you!

A man would prefer having a drink, a nice meal, and sex over talking about most anything. But he will talk if you let him know ahead of time that you want to talk about something emotional so it gives him time to tap into the emotional part of his brain.

You start screaming: **"You never touch or hold me anymore. Don't you love me? You just come home, sit your fat butt down, and turn on the tv!"** He will just say: "Whatever." He hasn't had time to get into that emotional room so he will just tune you out because he can't process what you are saying and when frustrated, just shuts down.

Keep in mind the analogy of the computer. He is slow dial-up so give him some slack and don't try to force him quickly into the conversation by intimidation or hostility as it just won't work.

You should put your hand on his arm (physical contact helps a man gain access to his emotions and jolt him into focusing), and say: **"Honey, I would really appreciate being able to talk with you for a few minutes about our being closer. When would be a good time to talk?"**

You need to tell him what the agenda of the talk will be (don't get into the details as that will just frustrate him) so he has time to process that information and tell him the talk will be short. Men cannot stay in that emotional room for more than 1 hour so relieve him by telling him it will be short. You can always ask for another talk later.

Let him tell you when a good time would be to have the talk. It should come from him, not you. He will not want to talk when he is tired, right after sex, after a business failure, or late at night. Believe it or not, he needs all of his strength to be able to handle an emotional talk with you. It would be like you just finishing a marathon run and someone tells you to get right back on the line for another race. He has to prepare.

Women say that men are "emotionally constipated." Interesting choice of words and they are probably right.

Women think that having talks about emotions and feelings is easy for everyone (even men) because women spill their hearts and souls out to their friends, relatives, and even complete strangers (watch the tv talk shows) at the drop of a hat. Men won't do that. It is too painful and uncomfortable for them. They feel vulnerable and weak talking about feelings or emotions.

Women don't understand how hard it is for a man to express his emotions so they trivialize it. Men don't understand how women can just spill their innermost thoughts out on the table for everyone to see.

"Most men would reveal themselves more if their words were heard as they intended them and not as interpreted by their partner. Accused of being hostile, insensitive, sexist, rejecting, or self-centered and getting a reaction of tears or threats to end the relationship assures men's 'closing up'."[8]

Men are very simple and poor communicators of feelings and their words are frequently misconstrued. "I learned that opening up to women is dangerous and rarely worth it."[9]

Take what he says at face value. Women want to read into every word, pull it apart, analyze it to death, and regurgitate it into some other meaning he never intended or even thought about.

The man says: **"I really love you and will show you that by touching and holding you more. I'm sorry. I will try to do better."**

The woman then says: **"Do you really love me or are you just saying that? How many times a day will you touch and hold me? The last time you held me close was March 11, 1998 at 9:13pm so I would give-in to your buying that stupid chainsaw. Will you do it without it leading to sex because you know how I hate that you just want to have sex with me all the time without talking and cuddling? Does love to you mean the same as it does to me? What's your definition of love? Give me some examples. I don't think you even know what love really is. And why don't you say you're sorry more often? Would it kill you to admit a mistake once-in-a-while too?"**

Sound familiar? Feel your blood pressure rising? Your man will be ready to shoot himself after this kind of talk and change

---

[8] "What Men Really Want" by Herb Goldberg, Ph.D. Penguin Books P.75

[9] "What Men Really Want" by Herb Goldberg, Ph.D. Penguin Books P.73

the subject or end the talk all-together. He certainly won't want to bring up anything like this again!

He already told you what he is thinking and your questioning appears to him that you don't believe him and didn't hear what he was saying. You became a nag after he tried to communicate with you. Stop analyzing everything to death and just accept that he shared his emotions with you. That is tremendous and he will continue to do so if he does not meet with frustration, doubt, or condemnation!

When you have a talk with your man, don't talk down to him, speak with a sarcastic tone, or talk to him like you are his mother. He is not your child even though you may think he sometimes acts like one!

Don't roll your eyes when he talks or give him dirty looks when he is talking. He will think you are rude and condescending.

Women can use 5 different vocal tones to express themselves. Be careful which tone you use with your man. He will become hostile, defensive, and critical if you use the wrong tone making any resolution impossible. Think about how and what you say. Listen to yourself. Sometimes it's not what you say, but how you say it that conveys the true meaning. You remember the different tones you used with your children to convey your message?

Women think that their men should understand what they are thinking without being told as that is how it works woman to woman. Women will finish each other's sentences and talk over each other because they know what each other is already thinking. I watch some of the television programs with all-women casts scripted to emotional themes and I can't keep up with their thoughts and words. They go a mile a minute without breathing and all of them seem to be talking at once but they understand each other. It just sounds like mass confusion to me.

Sometimes men can't understand what they are thinking themselves let alone what you are thinking! It has nothing to do with them not loving you any less.

Sometimes a man is not thinking anything at all! Did you ever ask a man: **"What are you thinking?"** He says: **"Nothing."** It may be true!

There are times when a man turns everything off in order to recharge his batteries and focus again. A woman can't believe that because her mind is always going at warp speed and she thinks that is the way it is for men too. She gets mad at him thinking that he just doesn't want to talk with her and is using that as an excuse. It may not be an excuse!

Don't expect him to know what you are thinking. Men like the direct, no-nonsense approach without games. Games are confusing and frustrating and men know that they always lose emotional game-playing so they don't like it. They like simple.

She says: **"Gee honey, I'm really tired tonight because I had to deal with a lot of difficult customers today. It must be the weather, full moon, or something. I'm getting hungry too because I had to skip lunch and my feet hurt because of the blister I got last Sunday while weeding the garden. It was such a beautiful, sunny day without any rain. The flowers will be really nice this year because I put extra manure on them."**

Why not just say: **" Honey, I'm really tired and hungry from a tough day at work. I would really love it if we could go out to eat tonight."**

In the first quote, the man has tuned you out about the time you started talking about the full moon. He became tired. He didn't hear anything after that. You get angry because he did not understand that you wanted to go out to eat (he did not read your mind) so you stomp into the kitchen and start throwing pans around thinking he is a jerk for not taking you out after you told him you were so tired. He is confused and has no idea why you are mad. The second quote he understands and will probably say: "Ok," get his coat, and you are out the door.

Be direct with men without criticism or sarcasm and you will get what you want more often. He will be happy doing it for you. He doesn't comprehend subtle hints and certainly doesn't appreciate being blamed for things he doesn't understand.

If a man voluntarily shares an emotional need with you, **listen very carefully**. It is extremely difficult for a man to do this as he becomes vulnerable and open to criticism and he would not say it unless it was very important to him. Since women want to talk anything emotional to death, they fail to realize the importance of the event and disregard it as the chatter they are used to hearing between females.

A man will only share an emotional need with you **once**. He will not keep repeating it. If he doesn't get what he needs from you, he will find it elsewhere.

Women misinterpret that if something is not repeated over and over again, it must not be important. They think something is important only if it is repeated as is the customary woman-to-woman talk. If you brush off what he says as not being important or have some defensive comment, he will not bring it up again but will remember how you acted.

He says: **"Honey, I know you have to bring work home with you once-in-a-while but we haven't been able to do anything together for weeks and I miss that. I miss you."** You say: **"It's my job and I have no choice. You don't want me to lose my job, do you?"** He was telling you that he is lonely and he misses you. He hears: "Too bad; find something else to do and leave me alone because my job comes before you." He won't beg for your attention and he won't bring it up again. He may find someone else who appreciates him because you just rejected him. Read the chapter about affairs. You may need it.

"Women speak an average of 6,000 to 8,000 words per day. Men speak 2,000 to 4,000 words per day." [10]

"Studies show that women typically make 3 times as many personal calls as men and the average conversation lasts 20 minutes. The average male call lasts only six minutes" [11]

Men think women just talk too much without saying anything useful so they stop listening. After a man speaks his 4,000 words for that day, he will just shut down and not talk. If you want to talk with a man, catch him before he runs out of words! And don't dominate the conversation. Think about how much you are talking and make sure your man has the opportunity to speak for the same amount of time.

Women don't know how to listen. Men hate to be interrupted when they are speaking as their brains can only think about one thing at a time and they get off-track when someone else starts speaking. A man can concentrate on one thing and block everything else out. Think of a caveman who could block out pain, weather, cold, or anything else in order to find, fight, and kill an animal for food.

Ever try to talk to a man who is focused on a tv program, trying to solve a problem, or looking for a bathroom? He tunes everything else out. Allow him to finish his thought before

10   Why Men Don't Listen and Women Can't Read Maps by Barbara and Allan Pease. Broadway Books
11   Excerpted from "Opposite Sides of the Bed" by Cris Evatt. With permission of Red Wheel/Weiser and Conari Press

interjecting. Women interrupt other women all the time and think nothing of it because their brains allow them to move easily from topic to topic. For a man, it is the height of rudeness to interrupt and they will only do it if the other person is rambling without purpose as they lose patience with mindless rhetoric. Sit back and force yourself to just listen without interrupting.

Women feel better after talking things out. Men feel worse.

Men are exhausted, confused, and many times frustrated because they did not understand much of the conversation. A woman feels invigorated.

If there is no action plan or resolution to the problem(s), the man feels the conversation was worthless trivia as men are goal-orientated. A goal must be achieved in almost everything. Make sure he is allowed to accomplish something.

Ask for his advice and then use at least some of it. Women use the advice of their hairdressers, girlfriends, and television talk shows before their own mates. Nothing is more frustrating to a man than someone asking his opinion and then doing the opposite because some stranger gave different advice. He will not want to talk to you again about anything important because you obviously don't value his opinion.

A man will joke and tease if he likes you as that is his way of showing affection. Women sometimes see this as the man belittling them. That is not the case. If a man does not like you, he simply won't talk to you. Period. He thinks that talking with someone he does not like is a waste of words and not worth the effort. He will ignore these people.

If a man stops joking and teasing you, it is a bad sign. He may have given up on you. Joke and tease with him too as that shows him you care about him enough to do so.

There should be humor and laughter in every relationship or it goes stale.

Never ask a man: "How do you feel?" He doesn't understand that. To a man, it's like saying: "How can we change the weather today so it will be nice?" It has no meaning or logical goal so why say it? It's useless jabber to a man.

Make sure you only talk about one or two things at a time and come to some type of resolution or at least a plan.

"You never pick up your socks and leave your toenails in the dresser drawer. I feel like just a maid. All I do is clean up after you. Last November, you even forgot my mother's birthday. And why were you late coming home last Friday? Dinner got cold and you know how I hate re-heating meatloaf and artichokes. And yesterday I asked you to pick up 2% milk and you got 1%. You just don't care about what is important to me anymore. You are so insensitive. Lois' husband wouldn't do that because he appreciates and loves her."

Do not jump around from subject to subject as a man will not be able to follow you. It's not that men are stupid when it comes to processing emotions or ideas, it just takes them longer than a woman and he won't be able to keep up with you. If he doesn't answer you right away, that is ok. Be patient. He is trying process all the information you gave him. Don't criticize him or he will give up and never answer you. Stick to one or two topics at a time so he can follow what you are saying.

"Most men can't handle an emotional outburst that exceeds 10 minutes."[12] Crying and screaming don't work with men. It is perceived as emotional blackmail. They don't

---

12   Excerpted from "Opposite Sides of the Bed" by Cris Evatt. With permission of Red Wheel/Weiser and Conari Press

understand emotional outbursts and will look at you like you are a raving maniac just trying to get your own way with this smokescreen. They will just say: "Ok, I'm sorry for whatever it is that I did wrong, again." You will get your false apology but it accomplished nothing other than delaying the inevitable. Be calm and rational when speaking with a man so he can understand the problem. It works much better and you will get a genuine response.

Use "I" statements with a man rather than "you."

"I would really appreciate it if you would take the trash out for me tonight because I can't lift that heavy can." vs **"You better take the trash out tonight or you will forget about it in the morning and it will stink up the whole house."** Do you want to get the trash out or do you just want a fight? If you want the trash out, use the "I" statement and he will do whatever you want. If you want to just give him a hard time and get nothing accomplished but raising your blood pressure, use the "you" statements.

So what should you talk about with your man that will stimulate and hold his attention? Anything he is passionate about. Nothing abstract. Ask him about his passions and goals. Men love to talk about themselves.

Most men are passionate about their occupations. Engage him in a conversation about what he enjoys most about his job. Ask him about goals and challenges he would like to accomplish in his field of work. Ask him what he has accomplished so far. Ask him how you can help him reach his goals. He will be taken aback as he is not accustomed to having someone ask how they can help him. He would love to have you help and support his ambitions. "Behind every successful man is a woman" is true. Men can accomplish miracles with the help of their women.

Many women are surprised and humiliated to hear about their husbands' accomplishments from other people. They go back to him and yell at him saying: **"Why didn't you tell me you won an award for your research? I found out from Kandi at the hairdressers today. I felt like a fool that they knew about it and I didn't. My own husband. How embarrassing!"**

Why didn't he tell her? Because he feared her criticism or even disapproval. He probably tried talking with her in the past about his research and she ignored him or even worse, put him down about it. How sad it is that men can't talk about their accomplishments to the one person they love and trust the most because of fear. And how ironic it is that men are criticized for not talking with their women ("He never talks to me!") when they try but are chastised for doing so. He wants to be your hero.

Ask him to tell you about his dreams. Men dream too! We aren't all Neanderthals scraping our knuckles on the ground! If you don't criticize or demean his dreams, he will open up to you. Encourage him to dream and accomplish those dreams. He will fall more deeply in love with you if he knows you support and share in his dreams. He will then feel a responsibility to help you pursue your own dreams and aspirations. What a great relationship: both of you actively supporting each other to fulfill your individual life dreams. That is exciting and inspirational! How can you both not be happy?

You can communicate with your man if you speak in terms he can understand. Be patient with him and appreciate that he communicates differently than you. He will communicate more with you if he is approached in the right way and you both will better understand and appreciate each other. It will allow you to better handle life's challenges and opportunities together without so much frustration and disappointment. Isn't that what life should be?

7

Men's Biggest Fears And Why You Should Know What They Are

Men are afraid of a lot of things. Really. They like to pretend to be macho so as not to look weak or vulnerable. Men hate to fail at anything and fear failure of any kind.

Men are afraid of women because they don't understand them and are intimidated by women. They know that women have the upper-hand when it comes to controlling relationships and men don't like to be out of control.

If you know what men fear you will be better able to help your man overcome those fears and he will bond to you. It is that bond that will keep him close and the more bonds you make with your man, the better your relationship will be.

Here are some fears men shared with me:

"Dying. Life is too short."

"Injury or failing health to the point I can't take care of myself."

"Death of my spouse or child."

"Failure."

"Not being able to satisfy my wife someday."

"Failure at the end of my life."

"Not being able to have sex with a variety of women on a regular basis."

"Losing the security I've worked for in both marriage and career."

"Being taken advantage of by someone I trust."

"Getting old. It's not what it's cracked up to be."

"Dying alone."

Failure of any kind is mentioned most often by middle-aged men so that must be the most vulnerable area for men. Men hate to fail at anything. That is why they are so aggressive when it comes to sports, their jobs, and going after a woman. Failure is just not acceptable to a man.

Dying is the next thing men fear the most. Death of a spouse or child would be the most horrific. They would rather give up their own lives than witness the death of their spouse or child.

Their own death before they accomplish everything they wanted to in life is also feared. Once again, it is that sense of failure before their job is done.

Being in poor health or disabled is also high on the list as men are fiercely independent and anything that takes away that independence is devastating for a man. No man wants to be an invalid dependent upon others.

Gently seek out those things your man fears most. He needs your help more than you can imagine. Comfort and support him so he can overcome those fears and he will fall more deeply in love with you.

8

What Men Like About Women Today

My survey of middle-aged men throughout the United States asked what they liked and disliked about women today. It yielded some interesting responses. They like women! Really!

They liked the fact that women are "more open than in the past."

Men like the direct approach as they are easily confused by multiple signals women send. Don't beat around the bush with a man unless you want to see him retreat in frustration. This new directness appeals to men but men don't like pushy females or females who act like males so be careful not to go overboard. They still want feminine but want to know where they stand.

"They are aggressive and smart. No more dumb blondes." So much for coloring your hair blonde, ladies.

"They work harder at looking good even as they get older." Men are very visual and need that stimulation to remain interested.

"They are more willing to give up sex without question. Although now I have to wear a condom." I guess there is a downside to everything?

"**They are more independent and willing to take equal responsibility in a relationship; financially and emotionally.**"

"**They are more adventurous.**" The word adventurous comes up constantly in my survey and talks with men. Men want an **adventurous** woman; not someone who stagnates and is boring. Men hate boring. You don't have to be a rock climber or trek to the Amazon but you had better be stimulating and open to new experiences with your man. Remember the word adventurous. Be adventurous!

"**I like women today because they smell good and dress sexy.**"

"**I don't like them much but they are fun to look at.**"

"**They don't depend on a man for a living.**"

"**They tend to be easier to look at than in the old days.**"

"**They are more forthright and to-the-point.**"

"**Their income potential so I don't have to work.**"

"**They are more willing to pull their share of the load.**"

"We don't have to be on top all the time now."

"**They are more intellectual and don't just wait on us hand and foot.**"

"**I like most everything about a woman...**"

"**Women have taken the opportunity to use their abilities beyond the home.**"

"They have breasts!"

"Very little."

"They are more honest and open about what they want unless they are your partner. It's still a guessing game with them. You are expected to know what they want without being told."

Men tend to admire women with traits similar to those they respect in other men. Independence, to-the-point, aggressive, smart, and hard-working are things men like and appreciate in women.

But you will see when you read the next chapter about things men dislike about women today, that if a woman is too assertive, she is a big turn-off. The secret is to find that balance between independence and "in-your-face" attitude. Above all, be a woman with all the attributes only women possess.

9

What Men Dislike About Women Today

Today's men like women who are independent; but not too independent. They don't like the "clingy" types who can't do anything themselves but they also don't want the pit bull who is constantly challenging them.

"I dislike it when women are too assertive and overbearing."

"Too much 'in your face' attitude."

"Those who feel they have to prove themselves better than their male counterparts in order to show their worth in the workplace."

"Women are too over-opinionated."

"They don't let a man lead."

"I have to wear a condom now."

"They are starting to dress and act like the prudes of the dark ages."

"They have an excuse for anything they wish not to do."

Golly, I thought that sounds like a man; doesn't it? Men can't do anything when they are supposed to!

"Sometimes they are too independent. A man still wants to pump her gas and change the oil once-in-a-while."

"They are too high-maintenance. Unwilling to try new things."

"It seems once they have you locked in, their weight blossoms." Most men don't like fat women; especially when they get fat after hooking you.

"I can't think of anything I dislike about women today." Sorry, ladies, I don't have this guy's name as I know you would want to contact him! He is one-in-a-million.

"They are extremely self-centered."

"They think that everyone (usually other women) are out to get them."

"Money hungry." This was mentioned many times...

"Too bossy."

"If we want to spend some time with the guys, they call us gay."

"Lack of respect for men. Maybe it's just the women I'm meeting."

"They just use their looks to attract us."

"They want to be treated equal but only if it benefits them."

"They are too obsessed with their appearance."

"They try to look and act like they're 25."

"They act like they don't need men and I don't like that."

"They cost too much money." Amen.

"Their 'I'm a woman hear me roar' attitude."

"Phony breasts."

"They're too domineering."

"They have to prove themselves to the world that they can do everything on their own."

"They whine about no free time but when they get it, they don't use it."

"They're foul-mouthed."

"They want only the 'perfect' man but aren't perfect themselves."

"Must have everything NOW!"

The constant theme I heard from men about what they dislike about women today is their over-aggressiveness. This also came out in their opinions of feminism which the majority said was detrimental to male/female relationships.

I know that you are thinking: "I could say all the same things about what I dislike about **men**!" But this book is about what middle-aged men want or don't want from a woman. Respond to my survey for women at www.cbrucewells.com so you can voice your opinion in my next book: "What Middle-Aged Women Want From Men."

You can argue all you want that some of these things men dislike are ridiculous but this is the reality and we need to recognize it and work with it.

If you know the "hot buttons," you can adapt and tread lightly. You may even manipulate these to your advantage in order to get those things which are important to you. Be smart. You can win the war without winning every battle!

10

"Swell. He's Having His Mid-Life Crisis! What Now?

Middle-aged men have a tough time admitting they are getting old. They go into middle-age screaming and kicking.

They comb their few remaining strands of hair over (comb-overs) to cover bald spots and then hope the wind doesn't blow them the other way. They can't see worth a damn anymore with those bifocals and their hearing is almost shot. They have to go to funerals every couple of days for their friends. They used to have Reader's Digest in the bathroom but now have "War and Peace." They get in the car and start driving but forget their destination, why they are going there, and have to stop every 5 minutes to go to the bathroom. It's not a pretty sight.

If a middle-aged man wants to buy a boat or sporty car, he is immediately "branded" as going through his "mid-life crisis." Some women look at a man's mid-life crisis as a joke and ridicule men who want some changes. They tell him he is being "silly" and he should just "get over it" and grow up.

Other women know the destruction this mid-life crisis brings to relationships and families and dread its appearance.

Of course, when a woman goes through her mid-life crisis, it is called "exploring new opportunities"; not her acting like a little girl with ridiculous fantasies. Recent studies indicate that about the same percentage of women have mid-life crises as men.

Middle-aged men put up with years of women's menstrual periods, PMS tirades which were denied by women, lack of sex because of "headaches", nagging because they were working all the time to keep up the lifestyle, and finally the mood swings of menopause. Men have felt excluded and abandoned for a long time because of the rigors of current family-life. They don't feel needed or appreciated.

I think most men go through a period or periods in their lives when everything becomes boring. Work becomes boring after doing the same thing for so many years. The marriage is boring because it is the same thing day after day after day. Even hobbies become boring after 30 years. Men need change, adventure, and challenges in order to remain vital, alive, and sharp.

Men also come to the realization that their lives are coming to a close and they haven't accomplished everything they set out to do. Time is running out. They are losing their hair, their kids, their testosterone, and their bodies. Men like to set and achieve goals and when they don't achieve those goals, they become depressed and set out to do new things.

I had built a successful business but always wanted to be a police officer. It was a dream I had since I was a teen but never really went after it. Finally, I heard about an older guy who became an officer so I went for it. Call it a mid-life crisis or just going after a dream. It took me a long time and much effort but I finally became a police officer. The job wasn't everything I dreamed it to be but I was able to live my dream and felt very fortunate to have had that opportunity.

If you want to do something, **go for it**. Living with not being able to achieve that dream is better than living with the fact that you never even tried!

How can you help your man get through his mid-life crisis? First of all, don't criticize or demean what he is going through. Saying: "Buying a sports car is just silly. We need a van, not a sports car" is an invitation for him to just go out and buy it today. It's like him telling you: "Why are you tired today? You just sat at home with the kids all day and did a little shopping."

He wants adventure so give him adventure. Find out what he has been longing to do and set up some mini-adventures for him.

If he always wanted to go fishing in Montana, get some information for him and encourage him to go. If he has wanted to be self-employed, see if you can help him start a part-time business without leaving his full-time job or if he can take a leave of absence. If he always wanted to go back to school to be a lawyer, accountant, or entomologist, get some college catalogues for him.

Encourage, not discourage, his passions so they can be directed and controlled. If you don't, he may run off to Alaska with some bimbo.

Never hold your man back with threats, lack of sex, or condescension. He will think it a challenge and most men don't back down from challenges. Guide him to accomplish his unfulfilled dreams.

Never give a man an ultimatum unless you are prepared for the worst. Men can't resist or back down from ultimatums as it would be admitting failure. Men will behave irrationally when given an ultimatum and you won't like the consequences.

A man's mid-life crisis is serious business. You want to hold onto him. Give him some slack and he will bounce back after this final stretch. The key is gentle support and guidance so he doesn't fall off the cliff of rationality.

He (and you) can survive his mid-life crisis with your help and encouragement! He has been there for you all those years and now he needs you to help him get through his difficult and challenging time. He will come out of it loving you more than ever if he gets your gentle support.

11

Computer Dating And Other Places To Meet "Mr. Right"

*M*iddle-aged men and women looking to find that perfect match after divorce or death have a difficult time because of hectic schedules, a multitude of responsibilities, and so few available prospects. It is also a royal pain-in-the-neck.

Who wants to go to bars looking for someone? What kind of man will you find in a bar, anyway?

Church activities and volunteer organizations are good places to meet but your prospects are limited as fewer people today have time for outside activities.

It's also difficult to get back into the dating scene at middle-age. You feel like a fish out of water. "How am I supposed to act?" " What about the yucky sex thing?" " What will my family think?" " Will I have to take care of him in the nursing home? After all, we're not silly teenagers anymore!"

The two most important things to keep in mind when trying to find "Mr. Right" are: you must put yourself out there to be available (and vulnerable again) and it is just a numbers game.

If you are emotionally available and meet enough people, you will find the right one. If you sit at home and go out to meet one or two people a month, your chances of finding the right man are remote; especially in today's fast-paced and competitive society.

Where do you find available middle-aged men today? You have to go to where they like to go and participate in activities they enjoy.

Of course, single middle-aged men have to go grocery shopping and I have heard all the tales of meeting someone in the fruit and vegetable section squeezing melons but what do you think your chances are of finding "Mr. Right" in the vegetable aisle just waiting for you? Pretty slim, honey. I never had a woman indicate an interest in squeezing my melons at the grocery store (maybe it was just me they didn't like).

Men hate shopping (see the chapter on shopping). Men are stressed out in malls because they can't handle all of the commotion and noise so that may not be the best place to introduce yourself either unless you want to help by giving us directions to the hardware department or bathroom.

Some middle-aged men like to go work out so they can try to stay "buff" so meeting him there is worth a short-term membership at a health club. Check it out a few times and see who is there. Men like the idea of being with a woman who enjoys the same things as he.

If you like hiking, frequent the trails where middle-aged men hike.

If you like swimming, join the Masters Swimming program that has swimming meets and you may meet someone at a tournament. At least you get to check him out in a Speedo!

Singles clubs can be meat markets but who knows who you

might meet? **It's just a numbers game.** Remember? The more people you meet, the more likely you are to find the right one. If you kiss enough frogs, you may come across the prince!

One other important thing to remember: **a man will not approach you unless you are alone**.

If you go to a health club and chatter the whole time with other women, no man will talk to you. You are wasting your time unless your sole motive is to get "trim."

Men are afraid of rejection and especially rejection in front of a group of women. It goes back to our high school dance (canteens or sock-hops) days in the 50's and 60's. Remember those?

I donned my white shirt and tie, discarded my pocket protector and was off with my mother driving me to the school dance on Saturday night in Feasterville, Pa. I was really excited about meeting and dancing with some cute girls. After a few songs, I would get up the courage to go up to a girl and ask her to dance. She would look at her girlfriends standing with her, giggle, and say: "No." I would slink back to my buddies at the other end of the room who are laughing too and nurse my wounds. Not only did I get rejected by the girl, I was humiliated in front of others. I won't do that again. Would you?

Look available! Look attractive, bubbly, and full of life. Smile and look like you are fun to be with. A man will not approach a scowling, grumpy-looking woman.

Say hi to guys around you. Ask their advice about new exercises you can try (men love to give advice about anything; even if they don't know squat about the subject). Make small talk.

If you go to a bar, go to a high-class establishment that caters to professional people. This is important not only because you want to meet someone decent but you need to go alone or at least be alone part of the time you are there. You will be safer in a high-class bar even when alone.

Computer matching services can be an excellent way to save time and effort so you can find that compatible match. Look at how many people you can check out at one time! It's just a numbers game.

The computer matching services allow you to scan many available prospects in a few minutes and narrow your list down to a few who have the qualities you desire. Who wants to waste time with someone not your type? We don't have time to burn today!

Make sure the computer dating service you use has a large selection of people in your area and shows you their pictures immediately so you can eliminate the ones without any teeth or Romeos posing with their shirts off! You know what you don't like so eliminate them. It will save you a lot of time and effort and you can concentrate on those who appeal to you.

Your picture is worth a thousand words. Men are very visual (superficial) and they must be attracted to you by your looks first and other qualities second. If you don't look attractive and inviting in your picture, they will move quickly on to the next profile.

They don't care about your intelligence, your wonderful job, your cute house, your dog, your perfect personality, your quaint flower garden, or anything else except that first visual impression. Men are shallow at first so keep that in mind. Make a good first impression with your picture.

Don't want to put your picture in the profile because he should fall in love with you for who you are and not what you look like? Wake up and smell the coffee, honey! That's not how it works with men. Don't be naive. "Mr. Right" needs to see your picture first! Stop the game-playing and get with the program. It's not the 60's anymore where you can wait for Wally or Ricky Nelson to call you! There aren't that many good guys out there and the good ones are snapped up quickly by smart women.

You need to put pictures in your profile which allow men to see the real you. Putting one picture in your profile where you are wearing sunglasses hiding your eyes, the picture is out of focus, you're wearing a silly hat, or makes you look fat, is just plain silly and you are wasting your time. Women who do that send the signal that they are not really interested in a serious relationship. The only guys who will contact you are desperate weirdos who just want a quickie or your money. You don't want one of those, do you? I hope not.

A man wants to see you close up with a nice shot of your face and a full body shot so he can see your figure. Don't be cute showing your pets, stuffed animals, children, grandchildren, or a beautiful sunset. This is not the time to be cute. It is time for you to show just you.

Unless you are an alcoholic and want a drinking partner, don't have the picture of yourself with an adult beverage in your hand at some party. You look like a cheap drunk. Look classy.

I have one picture in front of me right now that shows a 48-year-old woman cuddling next to someone with her hand on his chest. (Bad first impression) That someone has a huge, hairy, gorilla-like hand engulfing her shoulder. I can't see him but I have to assume he is her ex-something and am immediately turned off. Men don't want "used goods" and it appears she didn't think it important enough to have a nice picture of herself alone and inviting. She also says: "I am a carefree, independent woman." Wrong words to a man looking at you for the first time. It sounds as if you don't need him or what he has to offer. Never say you are independent; even if you are.

Take the time to have nice pictures taken of you **alone**. We just want to see you and the more the better without looking cheap.

Make sure the picture is flattering but not fake with too much touch-up. It should also be a recent photo; not one where you are wearing saddle shoes or taken at your senior prom 30 years ago. It should reflect the real, today you.

I set up a date with a woman who had a gorgeous, professional photo on her profile. I was excited about meeting this stunning woman but when I arrived at the restaurant, I encountered a frumpy looking woman who appeared nothing like her picture. I barely even recognized her and had to ask her if she was my date! I felt deceived and never asked her out again. It was a waste of my time and also hers so what's the point of the deception? Look good but not fake.

A few other things about your picture. Smile for gosh sakes! Why should I even have to say that? I can't tell you how many women put up pictures of themselves where they are frowning or have a scowl on their faces. What kind of guy wants to contact a woman who looks grumpy? Would you be attracted to a man who looked mean and nasty? Look nice and inviting.

Don't have a picture with glasses on top of your head either. I don't know what it is about a woman with glasses perched on top of her head but it transmits arrogance.

Never show your arms if you are muscular. I don't want a woman who can beat me up! And if you have flab anywhere, for heavens sake, don't show it in your picture. Flab is bad. Cover it up.

What kind of profile (description of yourself) should you use with a computer dating service so you attract the right man for you? What should you avoid so you can look your best for "Mr. Right?"

Don't lie about your age, marital status, weight, kids, interests, politics, religion, smoking, or occupation in your profile unless you think it's ok for the man to lie to you too.

What do you think the guy will think of you when he finds out you have five kids who are still living at home sponging off you, you are 10 years older than you stated, you put on 50 pounds since you had your picture taken, you smell like an ash tray, and you're a lawyer instead of a waitress? Aren't you trying to find a serious relationship? Be honest.

What **not** to put in your written profile? One profile I read said she was a feminist and if I was scared of that, I should get lost. Nice first impression! I would imagine the only men who replied to that profile were those interested in a roll in the hay or some burned out, drug infested hippie from the 60's who is looking for a sugar mamma. This is not the time to be assertive or arrogant. Be honest but be nice.

Don't put in a lot of negatives: things you don't like about men. Stress the positives about men who appeal to you.

Never say: "I don't need a man but would like one." I see that written in many profiles. Men need to be needed and aren't attracted to women who don't need them. How would you feel if he said: "I don't need you but would like to play around with you."

Never say that the man should like to shop with you, share his innermost secrets, be a good communicator, or be willing to commit. He will run like a scared rabbit. You know men hate to shop, talk, or commit so why set yourself up for failure? These things can be approached much later in the relationship.

See what you think about this profile: "I'm looking for someone who is confident, secure and understanding, not just self-centered. He should be strong, physically, emotionally, and spiritually and attractive. He should also be kind, caring, passionate, romantic, intelligent, responsible, spontaneous, and fun." Wow, she's not asking too much! What man could possibly meet her requirements?

Her first sentence was fine until she said "not just self-centered." That screams: "Most men I have met are self-centered jerks and you better not be one of those!" I'm sure she isn't the "perfect" woman either so why ask that of a man? Be reasonable.

Don't write that the man should be financially secure. All men think they are good providers and putting that in your profile makes you look like a gold digger.

Don't write anything that says you are passionate, sexy, or affectionate. This sends the message to a man that all you want is a sex partner. A man will not understand that you are trying to communicate your inner self as he takes things literally.

"Looking for my soulmate," "Grandma Seeks Grandpa," "Could You Be the One?" are other big turn-offs for the middle-aged man. He won't understand what "soulmate" means (does anyone?) and if a man can't understand something, he walks away in frustration. Middle-aged men who are grandfathers don't like being reminded that they are getting old. It would be like his profile saying: "Man Seeking Old Woman." Would you respond to that?

"Could You be the One?" screams commitment and that is not what a man wants to hear before he even meets you. He is looking for light and fun before even considering a long-term commitment.

"I expect to be more than just someone to fill your time" sounds bitter, condescending, and that you were just burned in a relationship. This is not someone we would want to start a relationship with.

How about this one: "If you don't have the same interests as I, you can bite the big one." She sounds like a warm, sophisticated woman to me. I'm sure she will get a lot of good replies. By-the-way, what does "the big one" mean?

I can't tell you how many profiles I have read which contained misspellings, missing words, bad punctuation, and sentences which did not make any sense. If you are not good at writing, have someone else do it for you. A sloppy, hastily written profile indicates a sloppy individual who doesn't really care about finding a mate and that's not the impression you want to put forth to a man. Think of this as your personal resume'.

Make a good first impression with your profile and pictures! Would you meet a man for the first time wearing old, torn jeans, uncombed hair, and bad breath? I hope not.

Here is the **ideal profile** that will attract a great middle-aged man: "Beautiful, vivacious woman with a sparkling personality desires a strong, confident, man for new life adventures. I enjoy (put in your interests but **nothing** about shopping, craft fairs, snuggling, or doing things with your children/grandchildren) but am open to new ideas with you. I enjoy cooking and keeping a warm, comfortable home. I may be the woman of your dreams and look forward to meeting you." You will get many good responses with this profile.

Don't think you are beautiful? You are the most beautiful woman in the world to the one "Mr. Right" out there. All you have to do is find him!

There are plenty of places to meet your "ideal" man. Be creative and adventurous. I am convinced that there is someone for everyone out there. Everyone has different tastes and there is a buffet waiting for you!

Make yourself available and remember it's a numbers game. You don't have to settle for second best because **you are the best**!

"Mr. Right" is out there searching for you right now. Finish reading this book and then go out and find him!

The Big Date

Middle-aged women make fatal mistakes when they go out on those beginning dates.

First of all, don't talk too much. You don't need to spill your life's history out on the first few dates. It's intimidating to a man as he will leave with the impression that you are a verbose, controlling woman. Let the man ask you some questions. He is trying to figure you out and as we know, men are slow on the uptake. He will also like the challenge of learning new things about you each time you meet.

You are not perfect so don't expect him to be. Some women even have the "list." The "list" is a compilation of all the things a man must be in order to make her happy. That is nice to have but do not tell the man you have the "list" or what is on it. He will feel like a piece of meat and will stop seeing you as he thinks he can never measure up to your expectations. Some women even tell men about their "list" on the first date! Not a smart thing to do.

The most important thing to remember in the beginning of your relationship with a man is not to take it too fast.

I know, you are thinking marriage on the second date! That is how women think. You want to pry every bit of personal information out of him on the first date to see if he's "the one." Slow down! Let the man ease into it or it will backfire on you later.

Men have no interest in talking about commitments, marriage (even talk about others who are getting married), or long-term plans until much, much later in the relationship. As a matter of fact, he won't ever tell you **everything** about himself so don't push it in the beginning of the relationship.

Studies indicate that the scents of vanilla and cinnamon arouse feelings of love in men. I do like vanilla scented candles as it gives me a warm, comfy feeling but I don't think of love. And I do like cinnamon buns too but I don't think of making love to a woman when I have my mouth around a bun. I guess if you want to cover all the bases, smell like a warm, vanilla cinnamon bun and men will flock to you! If that doesn't work, just eat the bun and watch a movie on tv!

A man will also look for instant chemistry. If it's not there, he won't call you again or he will only go out with you as long as it takes to reinforce his initial thoughts or just have sex with you.

You should look attractive and feminine. Smile, speak softly (loud women are threatening to a man), and act interested in your date. Ask him questions about his work and outside interests. Tell him those things you have in common. Don't tell him you love baseball when you don't. It will only be embarrassing for you later when he takes you to the game and sees you're miserable. He will then think you are lying to him about other things too.

And what about that excruciating time between the first date and when he calls again? "It would be nice if he called when he said he would call!" "Why didn't he call the minute he got home after our date? He must not like me! I must have done something wrong."

Men get caught up in their own lives and forget about making those post-date calls. I know, it's rude but that is how men are. They only think about one thing at a time so if they are overwhelmed by other matters, they won't call right away. It's not that he thought you were the date from hell. He may have really liked you!

Give him some time. Do not call him saying: "Why didn't you call me on Thursday like you said you would?" You appear desperate and angry. Let him call you or just send him a little note thanking him for the date and how much you enjoyed his company.

Sometimes men get distracted and don't call for a long time. They just don't think about how you are feeling. They then realize it has been a long time and are afraid to call as they don't want a confrontation and analyzing by the woman as to why they didn't call. They would rather not call at all than to go through an interrogation. This would again be a good time for a little note.

Do not call him. Be subtle and feminine. Don't try to intimidate or badger him into a relationship with you even if he looks like Robert Redford, Kevin Costner, or C.Bruce Wells!

12

"I Know That I Can Change Him"

*W*hy is it that women have this irresistible impulse to change men? It seems to be universal.

"He is a lying, cheating, boozing, drug abusing, woman beater but he has a warm heart underneath and I know that I can bring that out of him with a lot of love and sweetness so he will be my perfect man. I feel sorry for him because his parents weren't nice to him, he wasn't potty-trained until age 16, and no one understands him like I do. I know that he will change with my help."

Look at all these women who hook up with ax murderers who are serving life sentences in jail. They even marry them! What's wrong with these women?

"I didn't really notice his stupid baseball cap or ratty flannel shirt until recently and they really bother me. I keep telling him to get rid of the hat and buy a new shirt but he refuses. What's wrong with him?" You knew he liked to wear that cap and shirt when you met him so why the complaints now?

Don't waste your time trying to change a man because he won't change for you or anyone else. He may make some little changes like putting one sock in the hamper, but no big life-altering changes. **"What you see is what you get with a man."**

She is attracted to him because he is a powerful, aggressive, successful, businessman who gets what he wants when he wants it. He is the strong, silent type who can provide her with unlimited financial security. He is everything she thinks she wants. He is "Mr. Perfect." She hooks him and then decides that she also wants a warm, sensitive, passive, feminized, understanding man who will share his most intimate feelings with her every 5 minutes.

He should help her by vacuuming every room in the house, doing the grocery shopping, and will love to "brouse" with her at the mall for hours and hours. He will be home every day at 5:00 and all day Saturday and Sunday.

She gets mad at him for not changing into this other man she now wants when she knew what she was buying in-the-first-place. She blames him for not being what he is not and never pretended to be. He is bewildered and confused by her displeasure with him because he is the same man he always was.

It's not fair to punish a man for whom he is. Don't have "buyers remorse." He can't be all things to you and he won't change.

Feminists like to pick wimpy, passive men who will ask their women for permission to buy a pair of underwear or stick of gum. They love that warm, sensitive, creative, always dreaming kind of guy even though he can't hold down a job to support her and can't seem to get anything done. After they get these cream puff men, they decide that the men are too "wimpy" for them and get discouraged trying to change them to more "masculine" males. They don't know what they want, dump the wimps, and then characterize all men as losers so they can go on their men-hating vendettas. Men have been consistent in their desires; women have not.

Don't think that you have to "rescue" us from ourselves because we are so horrible and don't meet your expectations. We really don't need or want to be rescued. We are happy just the way we are. In fact, we thought we were just swell until you pointed out our supposed short-comings.

What you see is what you get with a man. Take the time to understand him and allow him to be himself without being judgmental or belittling. Decide if his qualities are those you want and need. Remember that he can't be everything to you. Just like you won't be everything to him, either.

With the advent of the liberated woman, women have changed; men have not and then women resent that men haven't become more feminine.

Women want to try "behavior modification" with men. They think that they can house-train a man like a dog and he will change to suit their new ever-changing requirements. Some even come out and brazenly say they will treat men as they do their dogs! This approach may change a few small things like putting the toilet seat down or throwing his empty beer bottle in the re-cycling bin and lead to a short-term modification, but the man will always go back to his true self. Men will not be totally feminized.

Choose a man who is suited to you the way he is. List your needs and desires in order of priority. List your "must haves" first. Come on. Be realistic now! I don't want to see a list of "must haves" that is two pages long!

If financial security is the most important thing to you, pick an aggressive businessman who will succeed. But realize he may be stand-offish and not home very much. He will be a "take charge" kind of guy who will make most of the decisions as that is what he does to succeed in business. He will be a little impulsive and arrogant. That is his nature.

In this case, your need for a warm fuzzy kind of guy who is around catering to you all the time must be at the end of your list. You will have to be a more independent type of woman who can function well alone. You will not get everything on your list so make sure you prioritize.

If you prefer a more laid-back kind of guy who likes to putter around the house fixing things, creating a cute bansai garden, making birdhouses, cooking your meals, and doing the grocery shopping, expect that he may not provide you with as much financial security as that may not be his nature. He is not driven to succeed in business. You will probably have to be in a position to hold a full-time job to help support the family. He may be comfortable not making a lot of money and that means not having some of the finer material things in life. You will have to make most of the everyday decisions as he will leave that to you. Understand that he will not be a strong, take-charge guy. He is not comfortable with that.

The bottom line to all of this? Don't try to change a man. Men don't change; not even for you.

Find a man who fits most of your most important priorities in a man and makes you happy. Forget about those traits which are not as important to you. Don't bring them up or agonize over them later. After all, you don't have all the qualities he would like either!

Does that mean you have to "settle" for second best in a man? Not necessarily. But you can't have it both ways.

Let your man know that you are pleased with him. Tell him you are proud of him the way he is. He will then go to the ends of the earth to continue pleasing you as your happiness is his happiness.

How A Man Shows His Love For You

*A*ctions are the only things which count for men. Words mean very little. Men judge themselves and others by their actions.

A man will tell you that he loves you and that is sweet and swell, but his actions will really tell you how he feels. He communicates through his actions and women have a difficult time understanding that. They think that emotions can only be communicated with words. That is not true with men. They hate talking about anything emotional.

His taking your car to the garage to get fixed and dealing with the mechanic man to man is his way of telling you that he loves you. He knows that would be difficult for you and that it will be a relief to you if he handles this for you. He just communicated his love for you.

Mowing the lawn or fixing the sink may seem like jobs to you but he is telling you that he loves you and will take care of these things so you have a comfortable home. He is protecting you from doing some difficult things.

He may just stand close to you without saying anything but he is telling you that he loves you with his actions. He is close to protect you. You can feel that sense of security, can't you?

When I do executive protection, the person I am protecting can feel my presence even if they can't see me. They know that I am watching for anything or anyone who may want to cause them harm and will intervene to help them if the need arises. They can relax and concentrate on other things. I also study my protectee's facial expressions so I know immediately if there is a potential problem. They feel safe and secure without words even being exchanged. Communication doesn't have to be with words.

Bringing home a paycheck and being successful in a job is also his way of showing you that he loves you through actions. He doesn't understand why you would whine about him not loving you when he does so many things for you. He doesn't think it necessary to tell you that he loves you when actions speak louder than words for him.

Don't keep asking: "Do you still love me? Do you? Do you?" He has already told you he loves you through his deeds so repeated questions like this are just nagging and redundant to him. He has already shown you his love through his actions so questioning him says that you don't believe him.

Recognize that men communicate through their actions and praise them for their efforts just as you would if he communicated through words. One man responded to my survey saying: **"Just once a week let me know that you appreciate me and what I do for you."** That says it all.

Tell him how much you appreciate everything he does for you and he will strive to do even more for you. He really wants to please you and show you that he loves you in a manly way. Half the battle is recognizing that men show their love differently than women. It's not better or worse. It's just different.

At the same time, if you equate these actions with the feelings of love, you will see how much he really does love you without requiring him to verbalize it.

Just because he doesn't show his feelings, doesn't mean he has no feelings. He shows his feelings for you in other ways and you need to appreciate him for how he is, not how you think he should be. He communicates as a man, not as a woman. He communicates with actions and those actions will tell you how much he loves you. All you have to do is "listen."

14

Feminism And Relationships. A Male Perspective

"Men are like roses. You have to watch out for the pricks."

"All men are rapists."

"Men are like teapots. Hot and steamy and done in three minutes."

"If they can put one man on the moon, why can't they put them all there?"

"Marriage is bondage."

"Women are unpaid prostitutes."

"Women need men like fish need bicycles."

"What's the difference between government bonds and men? Bonds mature."

We have all heard these jokes about men. Just silly jokes? Perhaps. Or are they malicious attacks?

Today's middle-aged men have been relentlessly bashed, ridiculed, and berated by the feminist movement since the 1960's.

Men have tried to adapt and understand this new philosophy that they are now the "enemy" and simply not relevant or needed anymore.

Most men have simply ignored the feminist movement saying: "Whatever." But it has been a difficult transition for men that has left marriages and families in shambles. Men are confused and angry. They don't understand what is going on and what their place should be anymore.

"In the 1970's almost 80 percent of men aged 22 to 58 performed 'that basic family role' (traditional breadwinners); now only 70 percent are among these 'hard-core employed'". [13]

In 1900, the divorce rate was 10%. Now it is 51%.

Things are not getting better for relationships and the American family, folks.

When middle-aged men were growing up, they saw their fathers assume the responsibility of providing food and shelter for the family. Their mothers were home taking care of the children. Responsibilities were clear-cut. Everyone understood what they had to do and, for the most part, fulfilled those responsibilities.

Today, women are confused. **"One minute we wanted to be liberated. The next we wanted to be taken care of."**[14] If women are confused about their roles, imagine how confused men are!

Men like simple. They can understand simple. Nothing is simple for men today.

[13]   "Domestic Tranquility" by F. Carolyn Graglia. Spence Publishing Co.
[14]   "Secrets About Men Every Woman Should Know" by Barbara DeAngelis, Ph.D. Bantam Doubleday Dell Publishing.

Modern men don't even know how to address women. Is it Miss, Ms., Mrs.? Women are hyphenating their names when they get married (or keep their maiden names all- together) so they don't lose their identity. Men see that as not wanting to commit to them by just taking their names. Some feminized men even hyphenate their own names with that of their new spouse. It's totally confusing for men.

The feminists then told women they should pursue careers and not be subservient, slave housewives. Raising children became an insult. Certainly not worth striving for. Men were supposed to encourage their women to get a job and then he should do housework, shopping, and be "Mr. Moms." Everything should be equal.

"I would leave (and indeed have left) a man before I would leave my career"[15] is the new battle-cry. Men today are just considered sperm donors and when science develops artificial sperm, men will not be needed for anything.

With the proliferation of sexual harassment lawsuits, men are afraid to even complement a woman. It is a sad day when a man cannot tell a woman she looks pretty without it being twisted into something perverted and illegal.

I asked men in my survey: "Has feminism helped or hurt man-woman relationships?"

Some men said feminism has helped relationships but interestingly also used the word "forced" many times. If you have to be "forced" into something, you usually don't agree with it in the first place.

"It forced men to see women's abilities."

15   "Get Rid of Him" by Joyce L. Vedral, Ph.D. Warner Books Inc.

"It forced men to treat women as equals. Mutual respect forms healthy relationships."

"It helped because we are more on an even-keel now."

"Helped because women know what they want and go get it."

Most men, however, said feminism has hurt their relationships with women.

"Women are more shallow now."

"The feminist movement was founded and perpetuated by a bunch of ugly lesbian men-haters. How can that be good for relationships?"

"It disrupts the natural order of things. Men are not adapting to the cultural change either."

"Probably hurt it to some extent. Anything said to a woman these days is easily taken out of context. A true, honest compliment about someone looking good can often be construed as a come-on."

"Men want to feel needed and in charge. I don't want a woman who never needs my help and I sure don't want a woman who opens doors for me!"

"Women use it to take advantage of situations only when it helps them out."

"I don't have a problem with equality no matter who makes the most money but the man is always the head of the household."

"It has hurt relationships. They are idiots."

"It has hurt as neither know what to expect or do now."

"Hurt because it makes men look bad."

"They just want us to be a bunch of pussies now."

"Too many women now with hang-ups. Money, sex, etc."

"Hurt. Many men no longer treat women 'special.'"

"Hurt. Men don't have an agenda other than food and sex. Quit trying to make one up for us!"

And other men said: **"Who cares?"** They just don't give a damn! The typical male response!

A middle-aged man today wants a woman who is self-confident but still feminine. Not a woman who wants to be like a man or act like a man. He wants to know that he is needed, appreciated, loved, and respected. He needs to clearly know what his responsibilities are and which do not conflict with his manliness. He doesn't want to be "feminized" or be expected to show his "feminine side." He needs to be a man, not a woman, and no amount of pressure by the politically correct police will change his nature.

The feminists think they have succeeded bringing women to the same level as men. What they have succeeded doing is bring women down to a man's level.

Men used to put women on a pedestal. Women were special. They opened doors for women. They gave up their seats (their lives) in the lifeboats on the Titanic. Men have less respect for women now. I know you see it everyday just like I.

Women readily give out sexual favors without asking for any

responsibility from men, they take men's jobs, the government financially supports women-led households as men are encouraged to abandon their families, and there is more male anger directed at women through domestic violence. Things are not going well.

A recent survey of men indicated that most would not give up their seats to a woman in a lifeboat on the Titanic. They would let them drown. Men are fed up, confused, and angry. Male-female relationships are going down like the Titanic!

Young women are angry too. They are angrier than their predecessors. I noticed this in police work. The young females were much ruder, more belligerent, and much more hostile than older women. They readily resorted to violence.

I went on one call where a young woman had stabbed her boyfriend in the chest with a pair of scissors. I asked her why she did that. She said matter-of-factly: "Because he wouldn't move out of my way." She then asked for her scissors back as she needed them for her job!

Vice-president Dan Quayle was vilified by the liberal "Murphy Browns" as sexist, bigoted, and plain stupid when he gave a speech praising two-parent households saying they are better than single-parenting. I heard the entire speech (not just the cuts by the liberal media) and he was right. Two parent, heterosexual married couples can do a better job raising children than any other structure. Witness all the screwed-up kids who grew up without a father around to emulate who provides stability and discipline. Now we glorify households without a father, gay lifestyles, transsexuals, bisexuals, and women who just want sperm donors.

Look at the television programs being aired today by liberal producers which portray normal lifestyles as abnormal and the abnormal as normal. How do you think that makes a man feel? Wanted and needed or just a necessary evil?

A woman can have a career and a good relationship with her man but she needs to put her relationship first, not second, to a job. She needs to reinforce that to her man because men lack self-confidence when it comes to relationships. Sure, men love sex but they are not all rapists as the radical feminists spew.

"Man bashing was so popular by 1998 the Shoebox division was Hallmark's largest selling division. Two hundred and fifty million dollars a year cashing in mostly on women's anger toward men."[16] Men don't buy cards putting women down. I can't even imagine buying a hate-women card let alone giving it to a woman and most other men would say the same. Can you imagine the backlash? Why do women do this? Because men are chumps and just take it (like a man).

T-Shirts are being purchased by mothers for their daughters which read: "boys are stupid, throw rocks at them." $100 million of these sold to mothers in 2005. If a man objects to this kind of male-bashing propaganda, they are labeled as being humorless idiots. That these t-shirts are just for fun and "why can't you take a joke?" is the mantra. Can you imagine the outcry if boys wore shirts saying: "girls are stupid, throw rocks at them." They would probably be locked up as potential terrorists and women-abusers.

There is a slow, deliberate, brainwashing of young boys and girls promoting hostility between the sexes under the guise of humor. These attacks on males must stop before relationships between males and females in this country gets any worse.

Men are blamed for all the problems women face. Feminists

---

16   From "Women Can't Hear What Men Don't say" by Warren Farrell, Ph.D. McGraw Hill

even say all of their problems started with, and are caused by men: **Men**tal breakdowns, **Men**opause, **Men**strual pain, **Guy**nocologist, **His**terectomy. Gosh, I didn't know that I was responsible for so many things which plague women! I feel just horrible.

Rachel Zoll wrote a piece for The Associated Press in 2004 about the Jewish reform movement that has left men not knowing "where they fit in." Females now outnumber males from summer camps to synagogues. There are more and more programs just for females so men are abandoning the reform movement as it doesn't hold an interest for them anymore. It is a striking example of how displaced men now feel in many areas of life.

The feminist movement needs to come back from the left to the center and allow for men and women to be themselves without the name calling, bickering, and hatred that has characterized this era.

We need to get back to valuing the traditional family unit along with appreciating and embracing the differences between males and females.

Men and women are not the same and that is ok. We are not equals in all areas. We can learn to understand our differences and appreciate our strengths and weaknesses without being so defensive and hostile. A few radicals have incited the war between the sexes and common sense needs to prevail.

We should be able to love each other as we are; not how others think we should be.

15

What Divorce Does To Middle-Aged Men

Divorced middle-aged men are a sorry lot. We all know that.

They really don't want to be divorced, don't like living alone, don't like cooking, don't like doing the laundry, picking up after themselves, and especially dislike having to shop. They are pretty pathetic.

Since 1950, the number of divorced men has increased by 8 times while the total number of men has only doubled. That means there are a lot more divorced men out there than ever before. It is epidemic and getting worse.

They feel confused, angry, and betrayed. Men can only think about one thing at a time so this influx of having to think and do everything themselves is extremely confusing. They can't think about work, what to have for supper, will they have a clean shirt tomorrow, or is it time to clean the bathroom because it smells like a high school locker room. It is just too much to process. They are on overload!

Divorced men die at a younger age than married men. Men need women desperately. It is even a matter of their own survival.

The suicide rate for divorced men is higher than married men and that is understandable. They are a lost and sad bunch.

They depended upon their wives to take care of these every day, practical things so they could concentrate on work, mowing the lawn, and watching football. Since there are so many available middle-aged women, men won't be alone for long unless they want to be.

Divorce makes a man miserable, bitter, and angry. Courts usually favor the woman over the man so he winds up losing half of everything he worked for and also has to pay the ex part of his salary for what seems an eternity.

If there are children involved, he usually winds up on the short end of the stick and has to beg to see them as his ex will try to punish him through his children. He feels like he has just been robbed and betrayed at the same time.

Don't try to get a recently divorced man to commit to another marriage right away as he doesn't trust women. Some women won't even date a man unless he has been divorced at least two years because he is "damaged goods." These are the same women who carry around lists in their pocketbooks with their "requirements" a man must meet in order to have a relationship with them.

Middle-aged men see women today as just wanting financial security without providing a man's needs and then blaming the man when the relationship ends in divorce. Second marriages also have a higher probability of divorce than first ones. It is a wonder any man wants to get married again in today's environment.

Men need to be cherished and feel important. If they don't get that, they will look elsewhere. When you take your man for granted, there are 10 other women out there eager and ready to steal him from you. Stop the whining, nagging, and neglect. Show him he is needed and wanted and he will be with you forever.

Why is the suicide rate higher for divorced men? It is because men cannot be failures. They must succeed. No matter what the reasons, divorce to a man is a supreme failure. He was not able to make his woman happy. He was not able to make himself happy. His family and children are disappointed in him. It takes all of a man's energy to come back from failure to succeed again and many don't make it. A man cannot live with failure.

Police officers see misery and failure every day. They see the worst of people and have to try and patch things up. It is an impossible task and sometimes that failure gets to them too. They start drinking too much so they can forget. Their suicide rate is double the norm for men. They are supposed to be perfect and if they slip up, criticism comes quickly and harshly. Failure is not an option for a police officer so they take the other option out.

It is a sad commentary about our society today that does not tolerate failure. Everyone is supposed to be perfect. We criticize politicians and movie stars when they make mistakes but overlook our own. Failure can be a learning experience and the most successful people failed many times. It should not be a life or death experience to fail once-in-a-while but our society today makes it so.

Divorced men feel they have lost everything: home, children, love, money, respect, and admiration.

"Divorced moms are five times more likely to make negative comments about dad behind his back than dads are about moms."[17]

17   From "Women Can't Hear What Men Don't say" by Warren Farrell, Ph.D. McGraw Hill

Don't be one of those negative women. It is destructive to everyone and accomplishes nothing in the long-run.

Men already feel like losers after a divorce and that is reinforced even more when his children are influenced to show lack of respect and admiration for him.

If you want to be with a divorced man and you are also divorced, keep your negative comments about your ex-spouse to a minimum. Middle-aged divorced men are very sensitive to negativity because of what they have been through and will gravitate away from negative women like the plague as they won't want to be with another negative woman. They want and need positive things now.

"Men leave marriages because they could no longer tolerate their wives' negativity."[18] This is very true.

Allow your divorced man the opportunity of experiencing happiness again and a fresh start with you. He will relish this opportunity and return the love to you in ways you dreamed.

He wants to be happy as much as you and he wants to make you happy! Appreciate what he has gone through and help him to become whole again. He will love you for it!

---

18 Excerpted from "Opposite Sides of the Bed" by Cris Evatt with Permission of Red Wheel/Weiser and Conari Press.

16

Why Men Hate Shopping, Coupons, And Self-Service

As you know, women are constantly frustrated with men for a variety of reasons. Men are just strange. One of the biggies, however, is a man's resistance to shopping.

Women love to wander around malls all day looking at every little nick-nack that is on sale and would love to have their man there with them sharing in this wonderful, exhilarating, bonding, experience. They don't understand why men abhor shopping and think men just don't want to spend time with them. "If he really loved me, he would take me shopping."

Men hate shopping. Most men in my survey responded that they do not like shopping unless it is for some "man" thing (power saw, golf clubs, new car, lawnmower, etc.).They would rather have a prostate exam with cold hands than go for a day of shopping. Making a man go shopping is like you having to spend all day in the hardware store. Painful.

Women think men are just being petty and mean by not going shopping with them. Sometimes that is true (we like to occasionally irritate you) but mostly it is because men are wired differently. Our instinct is to focus on what we need, go to it, kill it, and bring it home. Wandering around browsing at things is frustrating and frustration leads to anger and resentment for men. We don't like frustration. Frustration is bad.

How do most men shop? You know already because you've seen it a hundred times. Men figure out what they need (or what a woman tells them they need), go to the nearest store, run to the counter closest to the door, pick it out, and flee back home. **"I like to get what I need and get out!"** was the response men gave to shopping.

Men are good for about 30 minutes of shopping. After 30 minutes, they're finished and want to get the heck out of there.

"I know what I want to buy before I go to the store. No window shopping here!"

"I like to get in and out asap!"

"We hate to shop and talk on the phone so that only leaves sports, beer, and sex."

"Shopping trips with women make certain men highly anxious. We're talking BPA-Borderline Panic Attack."[19]

I know, you think it is silly for a man to have a panic attack just by shopping.

"Men are just wimps when it comes to shopping. It's a piece of cake!" That is what women think.

How do you feel when you have to go to buy a car? The salesman with the bad rug on his head, bad breath, and rotten, yellow teeth is high-pressuring you by expounding on all those meaningless things about the car that only men pretend to understand. After nodding your head like you know what he's

---

19 Excerpted from "Opposite Sides of the Bed" by Cris Evatt with Permission of Red Wheel/Weiser and Conari Press.

talking about, you have to endure: "I'll take your ridiculously low offer to my sales manager but I don't think he will accept it. I'm sure he will be mad at me for even bringing it to him." You too are out of your element and extremely uncomfortable in certain situations.

Watch a man's face and eyes when he goes into a mall or large grocery store. It is the deer in the headlights look. Women can think and process large amounts of information with both sides of their brains instantly. They can shop, talk on the cell phone, and do their nails with no effort at all.

Men only think with one side of their brains at a time. There is simply too much information coming in to process when they look at a mall. Too many people, too many stores, too much noise, too many screaming kids, too many flashing lights, too many things! It is too confusing and distracting for a man.

Confusion results in frustration and anxiety. Shopping can actually be bad for a man's health. Of course, if he has a large life insurance policy, it may pay you to take him to the mall every day!

I get lost easily in a mall and need a woman to guide me around and tell me where to go and what to buy. She will lead me by the hand like a little kid. I really look pathetic but it's the only way I can function in the mall.

Notice how many people hold hands in the mall. It's not because they are madly in love; it's because the men are lost and confused in this maze of people and stores and need the women to lead them around. Maybe a stroller for men would be a good idea (with a tv tuned into sports, of course). Just take his credit card and throw him in the stroller!

Ever send a man to do a woman's job? Send a man to buy

something at the grocery store and what happens? He comes back with everything but what you sent him for. Is he dumb, or what? That is because men are impulse shoppers. They hate lists (give one to him anyway if you want him to bring you a few of the things you need) because that would be admitting their memories are shot along with their hair, waistlines, and sex life.

Men will buy 50 pounds of steaks because they like grilling or 10 bottles of ketchup because there wasn't ketchup in the house when they needed it 5 years ago. They don't care if something is on sale or if they will ever use the item again. If it looks good, they buy it even if it's not on the list.

If he can't find something on your list right away, he will say: "Screw it!" and not look any further or get a substitute. Don't get angry with him when some things are missing. He can't help it. He doesn't have the patience to keep looking for that little bottle of green olives that is tucked away in the fruit aisle.

Never ask a man to buy you feminine products; he will be too embarrassed at the check-out counter. He will try to hide them under that package of steaks. He knows the check-out counter girl will give him a funny look and it is embarrassing. Men don't like to be embarrassed.

Some men do like to shop but not to browse. Here is what they said:

"I like to go to wine shops, etc. to learn more about things."

"I like to view available selections in order to make better decisions."

"You can learn a lot about your partner if you shop with her!"

"I like to shop with my wife so I can keep an eye on what she spends."

"I like to watch other people and see what's new."

"It can be fun to spend some time with your significant other doing something she likes."

Shopping must have a purpose for a man. If it is to learn something new about products (or you), he may want to go. If you find a guy who really does like to browse and shop with you, snatch him up because he is one-in-a-million. Of course, he may also like to wear your underwear around the house so be careful of what you ask for!

Men don't like discount cards, coupons, or gimmicks of any kind. Just give us the best price you have without the gimmicks! I remember collecting all those green stamps that had to be moistened and put into little books to redeem for a free toaster. My hands got sticky and wet and I always came up short filling a whole book. You then had to take all those books to the store, wait in line for an hour, and finally leave with something that will break in a week. It was pure torture for me.

Men don't like to be diddled to death about anything and will give up if it is too petty or frustrating. They like the direct approach. They get no satisfaction coming home and looking at how much they saved by cutting out coupons. It's not important to a man.

We also hate returning things. It was hard enough buying it in the first place and then waiting in line to return it for credit is excruciating. It is also admitting you made a mistake buying it in the first place. I have thrown things away rather than returning them. It was for my mental health!

Because middle-aged men don't have much patience for little things, they don't like self-service checkout lines either. I never go to self-service checkout even at the big hardware stores and I don't see many other men using them, either. One large hardware store I go to even has a female employee in front of the checkout counters herding men like dumb cows to the self-service counter because men won't go there on their own. We don't like the hassle. You try to ring the stuff up yourself and it always errors out and you have to go get someone to help you. Men hate to ask for help or directions so that is even more painful so why not just use the full-service lane in the first place? Even if they offered a discount, we wouldn't use self-service checkout.

We don't like long lines, either. We will just leave the stuff sitting there and leave if it takes too long to check out. Waiting for a table at a restaurant is the same thing. You better provide me with a good, stiff Manhattan and a place to sit if you want me to wait for a table more than 20 minutes otherwise I am gone. The only men left are those with women who insisted on waiting hours and hours because their girlfriends told them they just had to eat there. He would have left and picked up a burger.

If you want to get a man to shop in your store, stop building these mega-stores, make things easy for even a man to find, and have lots of open check-out counters (no self-service)so I can get out fast.

Most grocery stores are not men-friendly even though about half the shoppers now are men because they are single and have to fend for themselves. I don't want to take a 4 mile hike just to pick up milk and a jar of pickles. Have aisles marked with all the things in those aisle. Make it easy for me and I will buy twice what I came in for because I am a male impulse buyer.

One final reason men don't like to shop: women clog up the aisles gossiping to other women. I think they just stand there to aggravate the hell out of men; probably some kind of passive-aggressive pay-back thing for years of doing laundry and putting up with us. You'll see men moving fast down the aisles with those carts. We are there to get our stuff and get out quickly so don't block the aisles talking about Johnny's test grades last week. It's rude and annoying to men and makes an already agonizing shopping experience even more distasteful.

Help your middle-aged man out by not taking him on shopping trips. If he must go with you because his underwear have turned black and have holes in them from 30 years of use or his pants are bursting at the seams from the extra 20 pounds he put on because you're such a good cook, make the trips short. Better yet, do the shopping for him. Buy a tape measurer and measure him before you go so you know his size.

Pick the things out he would like and bring them home. He will love you for it. Then ask him to take you to dinner as the reward for him being able to stay home and watch the ball game. You are both happy!

Above all, understand that most men do not like shopping but it is not an affront to you. There are physiological reasons why shopping is stressful for a man. He doesn't love you any less. Help him out and he will help you in other areas and he will love you even more for relieving that shopping stress on him. You don't want him to shop until he drops! Do you??

17

Why A Man's Job Comes Before You

If you make a man feel good about the work he does, he will be happy. A happy man is a loving man. Every time you tell him that his work is important, exciting, and means the world to you, he will fall in love with you all over again. It is that simple. Men are simple.

If you constantly criticize what he does for a living, admonish him for being late, or just not talk about his work at all, he will become bitter and frustrated and refuse to give you what you want in the relationship. Why should he make the effort? You are telling him through his work that he is a failure and poor provider.

A man's job is the one of the most important things in his life because it defines his self-worth. He needs to know he is making a difference, is respected, and successful. Unfortunately, it even comes before women and family.

When a man loses his job, it is one of the most devastating events in his life as it tells him he is a failure and men cannot tolerate being a failure. Higher than normal suicide rates and higher divorces demonstrate the seriousness of this failure to a man and why it comes before marriage and family. For a middle-aged man who will find it even more difficult to find a job because of his age, it can become a matter of life or death.

A job helps a man feel more confident in himself and better able to handle life in general. A man needs reassurance from a woman that his life has meaning and value. He doesn't talk with other men about these things so if he doesn't get that reassurance from the woman he is with, he simply goes without. Women can get that positive feedback from other women; men don't have that support system. He desperately needs that from you.

Women are attracted to successful, professional, businessmen who are driven to make big bucks so they can have the "finer things in life." Even if they are short, bald, fat, and ugly, these men attract women in droves. You see it everyday in the tabloids!

Once a woman has snagged one of these successful men, she starts complaining that he is always gone, doesn't care about her anymore, and is distracted by his business even when he is home. She changed. He didn't. The man can't understand why his woman is giving him a hard time when she knew what he was like before they married and he is providing her with everything she wanted. He feels betrayed. He will tell her to stop whining and go out and buy a new pair of shoes.

With a man, what you see is what you get. If you want an ambitious, wealthy man who will give you a lot of material things, don't complain later that he is a workaholic. You can't have it both ways and men don't change.

If you want to compete with a man in the work environment, watch out. Men are fierce competitors. They hate to lose at anything and can't stand coming in second. They will be tough and act without emotion. For them, it is survival of the fittest and they will step on anyone in the way without feeling regret. Other men understand that and accept it. I see women in the workplace who want to take men's jobs and are surprised at how antagonistic men become and are surprised that they are not more sensitive and feeling like women.

If you are competing with a man, be a woman. Don't dress like a man. He will appreciate and respect that. Be direct and forceful without emotion, condescension, or cockiness. Be brief and to the point. Stand up for what you believe. Men respect the opinions of others as long as they are committed and logical. Men don't like wishy-washy, ineptness, or long-winded chatter.

If you realize and appreciate the fact that a man's job defines his self-worth and is not just a paycheck, you will better understand why it is so high on his list of life priorities and why he is so aggressive.

You want a man who is happy, confident, and healthy. His job helps him to be that man. Your support of his occupation is critical to his well-being and happiness. It is also critical to your happiness with the relationship. He needs your help more than you would ever realize and will love you more deeply when he gets it.

18

Why Middle-Aged Men Have Affairs–"What Was He Thinking?"

I have never met a man who had an affair and said it was because he was getting **too much sex and attention** at home or that his wife was **too exciting**. There is always something missing he is searching for.

Why do middle-aged men have affairs? Here are some quotes from my survey:

"**Lack of excitement in the marriage.**"

"**Because women become more interested in their own pursuits than working on their marriages.**"

"**Variety and stupidity. Mostly stupidity.**"

"**Lack of attention and affection and not truly appreciated by their mate.**"

"**Lack of sex.**"

"**When they lose that critical connection to their spouse's heart.**"

"No oral sex."

"The same old thing. Boredom."

"The challenge."

"Boredom"

"The inability to totally commit to just one person."

"Stupidity. Men think with their penis'"

"They're not appreciated by their mate."

"Men are supposed to spread their seeds."

"More opportunities because more travel in business."

"Stupidity. He doesn't realize what he had until it is gone."

"She isn't quite as exciting in bed as she used to be."

"A woman who sleeps with many men is a whore. A man who sleeps with many women is a stud."

"Novelty."

"Vanity."

"The thrill but it is stupid if there's even a remote chance of getting caught."

There is always something missing and he will tell his wife what that is long before he has an affair. She doesn't listen to him because she is conditioned to heed only those things repeated over and over again as is done by other women. If it is not repeated, she will think it must not be important.

A man will only tell you once or twice what his needs are. It is embarrassing and humiliating for him to express anything with an emotional need because he risks being hurt and disappointed.

Listen carefully to what he says that reveals his feelings. After that, you will lose him and will say: **"All of a sudden he just got up and left me to go live with his secretary."** It wasn't all of a sudden. You will say he is a cheating bastard who betrayed you but failed to recognize his warnings because you weren't listening or didn't care enough to listen.

Men don't talk about feelings easily and if they get up the nerve to tell you something on an emotional level and risk being hurt, you better listen carefully because it is extremely important to him. You may only have one chance to listen.

Men don't want to have affairs. They know it is "stupid" and readily admit that. They said it over and over in my survey. Lack of attention either through not having enough sex or not feeling appreciated were the main reasons men give for having affairs.

"Men don't cheat just because. They are driven to it by years of pain and unfulfilled expectations."[20] This is true. It isn't just a sudden impulse. It was building for many years.

So what are these unfulfilled expectations? Men don't like their women to change. In fact, they don't like anything to change. Ever try to take away his checkered flannel shirt he has been wearing since 1962? He loves that shirt even with all the holes and stains because it is comfortable and familiar.

He likes things the way they are. He can put on 100 lbs in his gut and can't see his belt anymore. His butt-crack shows

20   "What Do Men Want" by Hallie Poticki. Sourcebooks

when he bends over to pick up the remote. He doesn't notice that he has changed. In his mind he is still that buff 25 year-old with long hair and washboard abs. But his woman had better not change her appearance. He fell in love with, and committed to, a certain woman.

Remember how hard you tried to please him before he proposed? You wanted to look good to please him. You made him his favorite meals. You complimented him on his work, his personality, his hair, his teeth, and his dependability.

Remember how many times per week you had sex with him in the beginning of the relationship? How many times is it now?

Men feel they have been taken for granted. Don't let your man feel neglected.

When sex with him becomes a monthly chore and you just lay back and yawn until he is finished his thing.

When you put on the thigh and stomach flab.

When you give up make-up because "it's too much of a hassle" and the natural look should be acceptable.

When you change your hair color from blonde to black because your hairdresser said it was the latest rage.

When you go from long, flowing, sexy hair to a boyish-looking crew-cut because it is easier to take care of.

When you tell him that you are going back to work full-time and he will have to fend for himself because it is "your time" now. You changed. He didn't and he is angry. He feels betrayed and angry.

Remember the word betrayed because it comes up constantly when men talk about their disappointments with women.

Don't even think about saying: "You should love me for me, not the way I look." Men are visual and they love or hate what they see no matter what the logic or how much you try to intimidate them. He will say: "Yes, dear, I'll love you no matter what" and then set up a lunch date with a young, slim, long-haired babe who acts like she adores his "jolly" beer belly and his enthralling conversation about arthritis. He hasn't had this much attention since you were dating and he loves it.

After a hard day's work hunting and slaying dragons for his family, a man does not want to come home to a bitchy, tired, grumpy woman. Greet him with a warm smile and hug, ask him how his day went, and give him about 30 minutes to wind down. Do not hit him with any problems right away. In fact, why not meet him at the door with a sexy outfit and lead him to the bedroom for a passionate welcome home once-in-a-while? Too much trouble or you will feel silly? The other woman won't. She will treat him like a king and say you are just an old, miserable hag who is too lazy to take care of him. He is too stupid to know what her real intentions are and just enjoys the attention.

A man needs variety in a woman and doesn't think just one woman can satisfy him. He wants to see that you can be a kind, loving, intelligent woman and a different, sexy woman in bed. **"Conservative in the streets and wild in the sheets"** is what one man said in my survey and that could very well be the slogan for middle-aged men.

Give him the feeling that he is making love to a different woman every time and he will be totally satisfied. I know, it is stupid to pretend that you are different women and you just want to be yourself. It doesn't make sense logically but whoever said men's emotions follow logic? They aren't logical and it can be frustrating but understanding these illogical quirks of men can make the relationship better. You don't have to understand everything or agree with matters of the heart but you can get what you need from a relationship by compromising.

Remember that men don't have affairs if they are getting their needs met at home.

Never have a "headache." No headache should last 5 or 10 years.

Be the sexual aggressor every-so-often. Tell him you want to have sex with him desperately and need him to make passionate love to you. Nothing turns a man on more than a woman who wants him. Find out how often he wants to have sex and make sure you eagerly satisfy that need. A man feels a bond and connection to a woman every time he makes love to her and that bond needs to be reinforced constantly so another woman cannot break it.

Sex is also the way a man communicates his feelings to a woman and if she doesn't want sex with him often, it is a personal rejection to him and he will resent the woman and be receptive to another woman's advances. In fact, he will feel that he has been deceived into providing for the woman with nothing in return and feels no inhibition or guilt making a connection with another woman. He feels betrayed, angry, and available.

Women forgive their men who have affairs; men don't. A man cannot accept the fact that his woman found another man more appealing. He will not take her back because she is "damaged goods" and his pride is more important than the relationship. It is a double-standard but it is reality. Middle-aged women have almost as many affairs as men today but affairs seem to be blamed on men. It is always "his fault." There is no consideration for the years of neglect and disappointments he had to endure.

A woman will push a man into another woman's arms when she constantly punishes and shames her man, holds grudges, makes him sleep on the couch rather than resolving problems, does not satisfy him sexually, does not show an interest in his work, or is asleep when he comes home from work. If a man does not feel wanted, needed, respected, and appreciated for his hard work, he will find it elsewhere.

Ask your man out on a date. Buy him a little present (nothing feminine or cutesy) and tell him it is because you love, appreciate, admire, and desire him.

He will not look elsewhere if he is getting what he needs at home. It takes hard work and effort but he will be yours forever and you won't have to worry about "the other woman" coming between you.

19

Don't Keep Score Unless It's Football

"Women take a whole lot longer to forgive than most men, and they never forget!"[21] Men know this all too well. Women remember everything and keep score to see if they are behind in the relationship game. This is one game they don't intend to lose!

For some reason, women cannot let go of a man's failure to do something her way, say something her way, do something her way, etc.,etc. They have minds like a steel safe when it comes to locking details away for future use to terrorize us dumb men. They don't forget anything unless it's how much they spent on clothes or their ages.

Men are simple. Let's have your argument, I'll apologize for everything I did or didn't do, we'll forget it and move on with our lives. We like to get on with things. We don't like to dwell on things unless it is how much to spend on a new tool, boat, or car. Men don't look back because we can't remember the little things about the relationship.

Months or years later a woman will blurt out: "You only gave me a card for my birthday on July 28^t, 1974. I gave you a

---

21   The Complete Idiots Guide to Understand Men and Women by Lillian Glass, Ph.D. Alpha Books P.85

power saw for yours. And then you gave me that crummy foot massager on our anniversary April 17, 1983 after I made you a nice meal. You didn't even take me out that night because it was your bowling night. You are always forgetting the things which are important to me. You're just an inconsiderate slob and I'm tired of it. You can get your own dinner tonight and cart your fat, beer-battered butt to the sofa afterwards and sleep there." He will look at you with dazed eyes and open mouth as he has no idea what you are talking about. He can't remember what he ate last night let alone things years ago.

Men can't remember trivial things a week after they happen no less years later. A man thinks they are not worth remembering. Men become frustrated and angry when things put to rest are brought up again and again and again just to punish them with no final resolution. Men want resolutions and finality.

We don't mind getting beaten up once for something but not repeatedly centuries later. The past is the past. Get over it. Concentrate on today and tomorrow a man would say.

Women who hold grudges and keep score about everything alienate their men as men feel they are always walking on egg shells and can't relax. You want your man to be able to relax around you and be himself. No one wants to live with constant tension.

If you think he messed up on something, tell him so, tell him why it disappointed you, and then let it go. If you keep bringing it up, he will think you are just a spiteful nag and will tune you out. You know how men can tune things out!

Keeping score on everything and bringing up repeatedly in the future will destroy your relationship with a man. It is not healthy and will just breed resentment. We need to concentrate on positives so we can have a happy future together!

Keeping score is for football; not relationships.

20

What Kind Of Perfume Do Men Prefer?

Just for the fun of it, I asked men what perfume they prefer on a woman. Women spend millions on perfume so I thought it must be important to lure a man with a sweet smell and I wanted to see if we could help relationships and the perfume manufacturers.

To my surprise, most men said they prefer a woman not to wear any perfume at all! That's right. Go naked (the usual male response). Of course, men are not very observant when it comes to things like smell so they probably don't even realize that they are being attracted by perfume.

The rest of the men said they don't much care what kind of perfume you wear as long as it is not too strong. Strong perfume sends a signal to a man that the woman is overbearing, desperate, or trying to hide something. Not the signals you want to send. A light, sweet smell is preferred by most men.

"None. If she is wearing perfume, I think she is covering something up."

"Opium is my favorite."

"It doesn't really matter to me."

"Angel or Este"

"No preference but don't take a bath in it."

"Clean, fresh smell like soap. Not flowers or fruit."

"Something fruity."

"Don't pack it on!"

"Sweet Pea from Bath and Body Works."

"Liz"

"Charlie"

"One with a vanilla fragrance."

"Chanel #5"

A number of men said that they were allergic to perfume so you may want to go light until you find out about your man. You don't want him sneezing and allergic to you? It's hard enough finding the right man!

I remember a woman in college who was interested in a relationship with me who wore some cheap, heavy perfume. My immediate thought was that she was too pushy and demanding so I did not ask her out. It's funny how just the smell of that perfume formed my initial impression of her without my even realizing it at the time. I know, that's not fair. But we aren't talking fair here. We are talking reality, not the perfect dream.

You might want to try a number of different perfumes to see what works best. Just don't go cheap or put too much on as that will send the wrong message to men. You want to be light, sophisticated, and alluring!

21

What Is The Sexiest Thing A Woman Could Wear?

As you know, men are very visual (superficial). And according to women, all men think about is sex, sex, and more sex. Women complain about the sex thing but know this very well and want to look alluring and sexy to attract a man's eye so I asked men their opinions of what a woman should wear to look her sexiest.

After all, you do want to know what appeals to a man; not a woman. Right?

Here are some of their answers:

"A long sleeve white shirt (no tie) and nothing else."

"A normal bikini. No Thongs!"

"Sexy lingerie from Victoria Secret."

"Nothing"

"Something that covers just enough to stir the imagination."

"Crop top and G-string"

"A somewhat revealing blouse."

"Just a smile."

"A muscle t-shirt."

"My shirt, no bra, loose gym shorts with no panties. Accessability with positive intentions."

"Snug jeans but not the new, low cut style."

"Women can look sexy in almost anything."

"After a couple of drinks, who cares? A robe looks good."

"A thong, a cold beer in her hand, and just a smile!"

"A white blouse with just enough buttons undone to keep things interesting."

"Not too much skin showing as I like to imagine what's underneath."

So there you have it. Now you know the sexiest things women could wear to attract a man's attention. Have some fun with it and see what your man likes! Tell him what looks sexy for him to wear too! Loosen up and have some fun!

22

Why Bigger Is Always Better

I always got a kick out of watching the television program "Home Improvement" with Tim "the toolman" Taylor. He was always trying to make something bigger, better, faster, or with more power. He didn't care if he blew up something (including himself) as long as he had the opportunity of improving something.

Men have this fascination with size and power; especially the size of their penis'. They always want bigger and more powerful boats, cars, houses, or tools. It is a sign of their success in life and it gives them the thrill they need once-in-a-while so boredom doesn't set in. It also gives them a sense of power and all men want to be powerful.

As a police officer, my uniform was dark navy blue with wide, sharply cut shoulders. It was designed to show power so if I was in a confrontational situation, the other person would hopefully submit. Sometimes it worked and sometimes it just made the bad guy angrier so he wanted to fight me. Of course, wearing a bulging bullet-proof vest underneath, a big gun strapped to my side, leather gloves, wide belt with two sets of handcuffs (to cuff fat guys), pepper spray, nightstick, and combat boots didn't hurt either. I looked like some kind of gladiator! Bigger was better!

If you want to impress and keep a man, recognize that he likes constant reinforcement that he has the biggest and best of everything. He will feel like a hero and treat you like a queen. If you belittle those things of value to him or don't allow him excitement and challenges, he will find them elsewhere. Humor him a little when it comes to his fascination with size and power.

Did you know that when men use a public urinal, they always stare straight ahead, do not look around, and do not communicate with other men? They don't know if the guy next to him is bigger and if he is, that would be depressing so they look straight at the wall. How many men ask another man if he wants to use the restroom with him when he gets up from the table at a restaurant as women do? Right.

Never, never, (not even jokingly) tell a man that his penis is not big enough. The first time you say anything negative about his penis or the way he makes love to you with it, you will lose him forever. He will probably not show his hurt and anger right away as it takes him a long time to mentally process emotions (especially negative emotions) but it will come; I guarantee it. It may take time before you actually see him walk away but it will come. I don't care how mad you get at your man. Do not criticize the size of his penis.

Remember that men believe what women say; literally and immediately. You will not be able to talk your way out of this later like you can with something hurtful you said to a woman so be careful. Before you say anything, know that criticizing a man's penis or how he makes love to you will end your relationship and there will be no turning back. If you want to dump him, this is a good way to do it.

Do not tell your man that he is huge if he is not. He will know you are just lying. He will be insulted and humiliated. Just tell him that he satisfies you in every way.

Never refer to his penis with a pet name. Saying: "Can Petey come out to play tonight?" is a put-down to a man that tells him you think his big, strong penis that is the most important thing to him is a little toy thing with no value.

Remember that a man communicates with his woman through sex and anything that diminishes that experience will be the same as he not speaking with you. In fact, he may stop communicating with you when you treat him that way as it is offensive to him. He will also think you are talking down to him as a mother would. He doesn't want or need another mother. He wants a warm, sexual, up-beat woman who will compliment him in every way. If you treat him as a child rather than a man, he will act like a child and get back at you in very subtle ways which will aggravate the heck out of you (he knows what buttons to push on you too).

If he wants a bigger boat, a sportier car, a bigger house, etc. don't say: "We can't afford that so just forget it!" Say: "That's great that you want something that makes you happy! Now let's figure out how we can work together to get it." If you encourage his dreams, he will appreciate it and give you the things which are important to you too. He may even decide not to go bigger after some reflection and not getting resistance from you.

If he gets a battle all the time from you, he will just go ahead and buy the boat without talking with you. I'm sure you have had that experience! Men don't react well to ultimatums or threats. They will come out fighting and not care about anyone else because they have to be right and maintain power and control.

You can have your cake and eat it too by encouraging your man to reach for his goals and dreams. He will then be more receptive to your ideas because he is not feeling threatened.

Remember that (for a man) bigger is always better!

23

"Honey, Just Leave Me Alone"

Men need to be alone once-in-awhile. It isn't that we don't love you any less, we just need some time to re-charge our batteries.

For me, I like going alone up to my cottage on Lake Ontario. I enjoy working outside, fishing on a nice, clear, day, reading a good book (no self-help books as men don't admit they have any faults, of course), and grilling a nice, thick steak while enjoying a VO Manhattan. It is a welcome relief from the every day rat race . I enjoy having family and friends up there too but there are times when I like just being alone.

When my kids were young, they always asked me what I wanted most for Father's Day. I told them: "Peace and quiet." It was a joke but there are times when men need peace and quiet so they can re-focus on their lives, ambitions, and priorities.

When a man is upset about something or hurt, he just wants to be alone for a while. It is his way of dealing with the problem. Some psychologists say it is our going back into our "caves" so we can heal. For women, silence is a punishment; for men it is a gift. We are able to wind down and relax. We can heal. At that time, don't ask us: "What is wrong?" We won't tell you until we are ready. Our brains are slow and it takes us a while to get through things. We may not even know exactly what is bothering us until we have time to think it through. Just tell us that you love and support us and are ready to listen when we are ready to talk.

Ever notice how a man likes to do no-brainer tasks like watering the lawn, painting the railing, working out at the gym, or washing the car? It is his way of relaxing so he doesn't have to think. It is enjoyable. There are times when men don't want to think at all! That's hard to believe because women's brains are always going at warp speed but that is the way men are. They need time to not think at all.

If your man occasionally acts a little reclusive, just take it in stride and offer him support rather than criticism. Provide him a place where he can be alone to do whatever he wishes without interruption. He will be more refreshed and vital.

24

How To Compete With The Younger Woman And Win!

"Women in their 40's have only a 32% chance of re-marrying. Women in their 50's have only a 12% chance of re-marrying."[22]

In 1920, there were 104 males to every 1 female. Women had their pick of many available men and men were falling over each other to attract one woman. Today the ratio of men to women is about 1 male to 1 female. Compared to yesteryear, it's slim pickings out there for women.

First marriages for men are usually with a woman who is a year or two younger than he. Succeeding marriages are usually with a much younger woman.

Men get distinguished looking with their silver hair and weathered appearance as they get old. Women have face-lifts, butt-lifts, lipo/botox-everything, boob jobs, and the latest fad diet to try and stay young looking rather than just "old."

Financially successful middle-aged men are in big demand and are snatched up quickly when they become available. They're not on the market long.

---

22 What Women Want–What Men Want by John Townsend. Oxford Press

Single, middle-aged women have to pick through loafers, gays, boozers, momma's boys, Romeos, whackos, women beaters, bitter divorced men, men trying to get their money, and never married perfectionists. All of this just to find "Mr. Right." It is a daunting task and getting worse by the day. It's no wonder some women give up and just live alone. Who wants to deal with those odds?

On top of all this aggravation, middle-aged women have to compete with the younger women out there who want to take their men away from them. An older man is a catch. He is better able to financially take care of her than a young guy just starting out in life. He doesn't require a lot of sex (she will have sex with him until his eyes pop out, get him hooked, and then leave him holding the Viagara while spending his money). And the older man is more mature and worldly than the young guys. This is all very appealing to the younger women so they go after the older men.

Middle-aged men prefer younger women because these women still look attractive (no flab bulging out of those pantyhose, wrinkled chicken skin under the arms, boobs hanging down to the knees, crows feet eyes, etc.). The younger women are happy and blissful not yet having had to go through menopause and divorces. It is also a way for a man to recapture his youth by having a young woman on his arm.

Men don't see themselves as getting old. They want to stay young and vital. They think they are still 30 (in their own minds they are always 30)!

A middle-aged man doesn't care if women snicker at him as being used as a "sugar daddy." At middle-age, he doesn't care about what anyone thinks. He is having fun, she makes him feel young again, and he doesn't have to put up with an old angry female who is always nagging him.

So after all of this depressing stuff, how do you compete with the young "hotty?" It's easy. Trust me!

First of all, look younger. As you know, men are very visual (superficial). Looks are extremely important. Work out regularly and drink a lot of water (keeps skin younger-looking). Don't get too much sun that makes your skin look like an old alligator bag but do have a little tan so you look vital and alive.

Dress with current styles, wear makeup (not too much or he will think you have something to hide), and have your hair styled often in a current style. You don't have to look like a teeny-bopper but you can look younger. He wants someone who is alive and exciting!

Don't have any gray hair! Gray hair on a woman makes her look like an old woman and the last thing he wants is to be with an old, gray woman who makes him feel old too so get that hair colored. Any color you want, but no gray.

If you are overweight, lose it. Fat looks old and frumpy. Excuses like: I had 20 kids so what do you expect?, I thought I lost 180 pounds when I got divorced, I just finished menopause, I'm retaining water, my cat died and I'm depressed, I'm waiting for the next fad diet, a Democrat won the election, the grocery store ran out of Slimfast, I'm big-boned, I'm still an 8 if I hold my breath, my exercise bike had a flat tire, etc.") don't cut it.

Men don't care about excuses. They just want to see the finished product and right now! Get in shape. Invest in exercise equipment or a membership at a club and work out. Whatever it takes.

The most attractive women I have seen are those who are in good shape no matter what their age. They look and act young and that is appealing to a man. I used to work out at a gym where a woman in her late 60's also came to work out. She was in excellent shape and was always smiling and made a point of talking and teasing with me. We had great fun and enjoyed each other's company while working out. She would be a great catch for a man of any age. Be that woman and you won't have to worry about younger women! They can't compete with a young-acting, mature, experienced, confident, happy woman.

Be spontaneous. Younger women don't have as many inhibitions and are more spontaneous and less reserved. Men like spontaneity and an air of freedom. It keeps them on their toes. Of course, be spontaneous about things he likes, **not: "Let's go to the mall and shop until it closes!"** How about whispering: **"Come upstairs and take a shower with me and make love to me after I get you lathered up!"** Or perhaps: **"I know how you love baseball. It's a beautiful day; why don't we sneak away to the game this afternoon?"** After a few spontaneous episodes, he will be putty in your hands.

Laugh and joke with your man. Older women today have lost their sense of humor and see everything as a serious life-ending drama. They have been beaten up by life and act that way too. They don't joke around or find anything humorous. They have become drama queens. That came up repeatedly in my survey of middle-aged men throughout the United States. Loosen up! You should be fun to be with and he will think of you as being young and adventurous no matter what your age..

Never say anything derogatory about men in general: **"Men are just after one thing."** or **"Men today don't know how to treat a woman."** A man will take this personally and think you are just an old, bitter, man-hater and he will steer clear of you. Think whatever you want but keep it to yourself.

When you walk, walk young. Don't trudge along shuffling your feet, looking down, or hunched over. Stand erect and confident.

Walk sexy with your hips swaying a little. You worked hard getting in shape and looking beautiful so exude that confidence.

Make eye contact with men without saying anything (that drives a man crazy). Look at how Catherine Zeta-Jones walks. How she looks at you without saying anything. Nicole Kidman has that same look. That look bonds me to them immediately. It touches my soul. Their look reflects an innocence and openness that invites you into their world. No man will approach you if you look unapproachable. Look inviting and a little vulnerable.

Match his sex drive and make sure he knows that you love to have sex with him. Younger women encourage sex and that is what you should do too. Read the chapter "Can't He Think About Anything But Sex?" to better understand why sex is so important for a man. It is his way of communicating with a woman, bonding with her, and being satisfied with the relationship. If you are not matching him sexually, you can forget about the relationship going anywhere. **If you don't satisfy your man sexually, he will not continue to love you.** I know that sounds harsh but it is reality and we're dealing with reality here.

Give your man a goal and a challenge. Men love both.

They love setting and achieving goals; even small ones. If he likes running and has dreamed of being in a race, tell him you would support him entering a marathon next year. You will help him train, make nutritious meals, ride a bike next to him, and be his timer. The challenge will be to finish in the top half of those competing. You are participating and supporting his dreams and he will love it.

He will also encourage you to set goals and challenges so humor him by doing so. The inclination of middle-aged women is to say: **"Why would you want to do THAT?"** when he tries to set goals and challenges. Don't be the old, negative complainer.

Participate. Encourage. He will love you for it.

A man would really prefer to be with a woman close to his age. She is more in tuned with his era.

She grew up with the same music, the same tv programs, the same politicians, the same type of upbringing, the same cars, etc. He doesn't have to explain who Milton Berle was or American Bandstand. She lived it too. He doesn't have to make excuses for going to bed at 9pm or getting up every hour to go to the bathroom. He doesn't have to pretend that he is 30.

But he will "settle" for a younger woman because there are so few middle-aged women out there who are willing to make an effort to "act" young and vital rather than old and bitter.

Be that "young" woman to him and you will have him forever.

He wants a young-acting woman; not a young girl. Don't sell yourself short or worry about competing with the younger woman.

You have so much more to offer than these inexperienced girls roaming out there for an older man to take care of them. You are mature and worldly, have taken care of yourself, are fun to be with, challenging, vital, supportive, and love him as no younger woman can. No one can compete with you!

25

"I'm Always In A No-Win Situation"

Here are the 5 top things men understand about women:

1.
2.
3.
4.
5.

Don't see anything listed? That's because men don't understand women at all! You don't understand us either. It's total confusion!

For some reason, women like to put men in no-win situations all the time. Men don't understand that. It certainly keeps a man off balance and feeling like he cannot do anything right. I'm not sure why this makes a woman feel better but it certainly makes a man feel angry, frustrated, and uncooperative in the future.

I volunteer to do the dishes after dinner to help out because I'm nice (aren't all men?) and want to be a modern-kind-of-guy who holds up his end of the housework. I always want to do the "politically correct" thing. It is a pain in the butt and I hate washing dishes but do it anyway thinking I'm helping out.

She says: **"Oh, that's nice Bruce, thanks for your help. You're so wonderful! But make sure you use enough soap, scrub a little harder as some of the dishes weren't totally clean the last time you washed them, and do the pots for a change. Would it kill you to dry them too?"**

My blood pressure is starting to rise thinking: "I'm doing this out of the goodness of my newly feminized heart and she's already bitching and finding fault." I finish all the dishes (and the pots too, of course) and put them away. Everything looks good enough to me so I go into the living room to relax and curl up with my remote.

She then screams from the kitchen: **"Look at the grease on this plate! I knew you wouldn't use enough soap. Didn't I tell you to use more soap this time? And you put the salad bowl away in the wrong place. I should have just done the dishes myself! Men can't do anything right in the kitchen."**

How do you think I will react to that? You're right! That will be the last time I do the dishes and she will whine in the future to her girlfriends during one of their gossip marathons that I don't do enough around the house. I don't care. I can't win. "Whatever" is now part of a man's everyday vocabulary.

If a man opens up emotionally to a woman and she puts him down because he didn't word it right, he will not open up again. This leads to a situation where the woman criticizes him for not showing his emotions or being more open. He's not showing enough of his "feminine side." He can't win.

Today's women want dependence and independence at the same time. They "want it all." This creates a no-win situation for the man as he doesn't know when he is overstepping his bounds helping a woman.

Remember when men used to open doors for women? Or when they gave up their seats on a bus for a woman? Not anymore. After years of snickers and outright hostility by women, men decided not to do the small things anymore rather than risking being in a no-win situation. It's easier. Men like easy. "She can get the door herself. Who cares?"

The same thing for complementing a woman on her looks. Saying: **"You look really attractive today. Is that a new dress?"** Thanks to lawyers and the radical feminists, even talking to a woman today could be construed as sexual harassment so why take the chance? She would probably say: **"Thanks, but I have worn this dress many times before and you never noticed. And does that mean that I didn't look attractive yesterday so you think I'm ugly?"** No-win.

Men have had to become eunuchs in order to appease the politically correct watchdogs. Castrated and docile. And then women complain that they can't find a "real man" anymore. No-win.

Men have to win or at least think they did. If you always put him in no-win situations, he will shut down.

If he volunteers to do the dishes and they aren't done just the way you want them, forget it. Complement him on helping you. Don't go behind him after he put the dishes away, re-arranging them to your specifications. Let him think that he did everything perfectly. He will be happy to do more for you in the future and you can guide him to do things your way through compliments rather than criticism.

No-win situations make everyone unhappy, frustrated, and miserable. We want win-win for everyone!

26

"He Just Doesn't Care About Anything"

"Women tend to ruminate over worries. Some women resent men for not worrying about other's problems as much as they do".[23]

Men act like they really don't care about much because caring makes them vulnerable and men can't tolerate being vulnerable.

Men don't care about self-reflection. They don't care about what others think. They don't care about other people's problems. They care about their jobs and being respected. They care about protecting their mates and their children. They don't give a damn about much else except sex, sports, and food.

Women get frustrated with men because men don't need approval before making decisions. Men concentrate on themselves and their objectives and can block everything else out. Try talking to a man when he is concentrating on something. It's like talking to the wall.

Men make decisions fast and don't think about how the actions will affect others. If they think it is the right decision for

[23] Excerpted from "Opposite Sides of the Bed" by Cris Evatt with permission of Red Wheel/Weiser and Conari Press.

them, they make it and will live or die with the consequences. That may be hard for women to understand but that is how men are. They won't change. Men are men.

Men tend to look at the overall picture of things and don't care about the details. They get frustrated when women want to analyze, ponder, discuss, and dissect the heck out of the details over and over again because the details don't matter to men.

Men focus on getting something done quickly, not in how it is accomplished. Results are what counts for men, not the details leading up to it. Just like talking with a man; he needs closure on the topic, not constant jabbering which men find useless and a waste of time.

"Women study men much more carefully than men study women."[24] Men are very superficial. Surprised? I don't think so! They believe what they see and take most things, especially matters of the heart, at face value. Because of that, they are easily manipulated by women who can analyze emotional situations and use them to their advantage. A man is just plain stupid when it comes to anything emotional.

If a woman tells a man that she loves sex and wants it all the time, he believes her. He doesn't think she is after anything else or that she will change in the future. He just believes her because she wouldn't say it if she didn't mean it. He believes what a woman tells him at face value. No hidden agendas or motives.

Men don't think about remembering anniversaries, birthdays, your first date, your first kiss, or anything else on an emotional level. Men are the brunt of countless jokes about having to buy flowers and chocolates because they forgot their wive's birthdays or anniversaries. Isn't that so?

---

24   "What Do Men Want" by Hallie Potocki–Sourcebooks,

Women think men are just unsentimental fools who don't care about anything but themselves. That's not true. They care about sex and football! Really, men concentrate on concrete ideas, not emotions so it is difficult for them to remember emotional happenings.

A woman can remember her first kiss 30 years ago, what color dress she was wearing, the style of her hair, and the color of her lipstick. A man can't remember what he ate for breakfast yesterday let alone all that old stuff. He is concentrating on surviving today and setting goals for tomorrow. Yesterday is in the past and the past is the past.

Men don't notice details. They won't notice that you got your hair cut or styled until two weeks later. They won't notice the dirty socks lying on the floor or the mud they tracked through the living room. The male species had to scan for food and enemies and did not care about how his cave looked. He had more important things to worry about and that consumed his thoughts. He worried about survival.

As a police officer, I had to work hard to notice details on calls for assistance. When I came into a room, I had to take in everything quickly because it could be important for my welfare and the report I might have to make later.

As a man, it is difficult to notice little things. Women can do this easily. They can instantly see every detail in the room from the style and color of the curtains to the paintings on the wall and will remember it for 10 years! I notice what is playing on the tv.

If you have ever been with an off-duty police officer, you will be annoyed at him because he is always scanning the area and people in it. You will think he doesn't care about you as he appears distracted. He is concentrating on possible threats;

things which appear not right. Someone looking like they are about to do something bad.

I remember getting a police call and going into a small room in a dilapidated boarding house where a guy with a mental disorder was out of control. I was talking with him and scanning the room at the same time when I saw a big kitchen knife on a small table near him. I got between him and the knife, picked it up behind my back, and allowed another officer behind me to take it out of my hand. Had I not seen the knife, he may have grabbed it in an instant of rage and stabbed me to death. My survival depended upon noticing little things. Even today, I notice things out of place that escape most other guys because I trained myself to overcome this deficiency. (I still don't remember birthdays) It's not that men don't care about the details, they just concentrate on bigger things. It's their nature.

So the next time you get upset with your man because he didn't remember your first date, it's not because he loves you any less. He is programmed differently to tackle large issues which he perceives to be more important and can only handle a limited amount of information. The small things get pushed aside. Give him a little slack and don't take it personally. He still loves you!

27

Men Need Respect

I created a separate little chapter on respect as men said the need for respect was one of the most important things they need in life (after sex, of course).

Americans have become progressively less respectful of others over the past 50 years. I'm sure you see it too in your everyday life.

There is a lack of respect for our leaders. Just listen to the Michael Moore's and Harry Belefonte's out there spewing their venom. It is beyond disagreements. It is hatred and lack of respect. No one talked that way 50 years ago. It was unacceptable. Look at the garbage on television and in the movies today! No respect.

There is also lack of respect for our elderly. They are warehoused and ridiculed for their senility rather than appreciated for their experience and knowledge. They are discriminated against in jobs even though they are the more loyal and dependable than the younger generations of spoiled kids coming through.

The lack of respect for parents is epidemic. Just hearing how young people talk to their parents with their screaming obscenities and petty, selfish demands is beyond comprehension to those of us in middle-age. Can you imagine talking to your parents that way? And our legal and social worker government bureaucracy has taken the parenting power away from parents and hijacked it. It is no wonder these kids are messed up.

I remember going on a police call from a teenager who told the dispatcher he was being "abused" by his parents. When I got to the home, the parents were sitting in fear while the boy was lounging on the couch. I asked the boy why he called the police. He said: "Because my parents told me I had to clean my room and I don't want to. They are abusing me!" The word "abused" is one of the most abused words in our vocabulary today.

I asked the boy who paid for his housing, food, and clothes. He said his parents did. I then told him: "Then shut up and clean your room. You are a spoiled brat and don't call the police again unless you are really in trouble. You do what your parents tell you to do and don't mouth off to them."

He gave me that "whatever" look. His parents looked like a 100 pound weight had been lifted off their shoulders. Government agencies should stay out of parenting unless there is extreme abuse.

One female in her 20's I stopped for speeding and cutting people off screamed at me: "I'm in no mood for this and if you're going to give me a ticket, you'll have to follow me home as I'm in a hurry." Another used the "F" word with me when I gave her a speeding ticket and even got out of her car and came after me in the middle of the highway. Would you have done this when stopped by a police officer when you were in your 20's?

A man needs respect more than anything else. He needs to be respected for taking care of his family and for the work he does.

"Most of the women who complain that they are not getting what they want from their husbands should stop and look at how disrespectful and disdainful they are of them."[25]

Men are no longer respected for being good fathers, husbands, and breadwinners; things men always thought extremely important. They are only respected if they are famous or make a lot of money. Look at all the movie stars or successful business executives who don't relate or care about their children. Or the ones who have multiple ex-wives. They are still glorified no matter what they do. The Ward Cleavers and Jim Andersons of the world are no more because they are held in contempt by the modern woman's movement.

"More men than women say their wife is their best friend. Market research asked with whom would you like to be stuck with on an island. Husbands named their wives. Wives named Mel Gibson or their best girlfriend."[26]

How do you think that makes a man feel? Respected and loved?

If you constantly let your man know that you respect him for who he is and everything he does for you, he will love you more deeply as he hungers for that respect. He is nurtured by respect and needs that for his survival and happiness.

---

[25] "The Proper Care and Feeding of Husbands" by Dr. Laura Schlessinger. Harper Collins. IntroXV1.

[26] "Everything You Know About Love and Sex is Wrong" by Pepper Shcwartz, Ph.D. Berkley Publishing Group P.7–8.

Men Need To Be Needed

"Not to be needed is a slow death for a man."[27] This is absolutely true. Men need to be needed in order to validate their worth.

Our society now glorifies single mothers, in-vitro fertilization, gay marriage, and job over family.

Men are portrayed as being irrelevant and useless. After years of this vilification, men are abandoning their wives and children in droves because they no longer feel needed or appreciated.

I asked men: "What's the worst thing a woman could say to you?" The most common thing (besides "I'm pregnant") men said was not be needed anymore.

Women who profess their strength and independence turn a man off because a man wants and needs to be needed. Don't think you are doing a man a favor by showing him he is not needed. Men don't want overly needy women who can't do anything for themselves but they also don't want someone who can do everything herself. Show your man that you need him. Tell him that you need him.

A man will gripe when his mate asks him to replace the leaking trap under the sink but he feels good at the same time

---

27   Men are From Mars, Women are From Venus by John Gray, Ph.D. Harper Collins

knowing he is needed for something rather than just a meal ticket. A man's actions, not words, show his feelings for others. He communicates through his actions and if he is needed to do something, it helps him to communicate those feelings.

Even if you can replace that trap under the sink yourself, tell your mate: "Honey, I need your help because the sink is leaking and I don't know what to do. The water is going to ruin the cabinet. Could you please look at it for me?" Don't say: "Bruce, the sink has been leaking for a week and if you don't get your lazy butt in gear, I will fix it myself or call a plumber and give you the bill." That is a recipe for disaster.

Your man has to be needed by you in order for him to remain whole and vital. It is his food. His very life depends on it.

Men Are Visual

Why do women dress provocatively? Because they know men are very visual. They will notice an attractive woman instantly, want to have sex with her, and they don't care if she is an airhead with the personality of a rock.

Women tell us we are just too superficial and that is correct. At least initially. A beautiful woman will turn our heads and get us excited.

Physical attraction is the most important thing to first attract a man. Personality and intelligence come after that. The first visual impression you make with a man is the most important time of your relationship. Don't ruin it by thinking he should love you for who you are; not what you look like. That's just not the way it is.

There are many women who don't put their pictures on their profiles when they try the computer dating programs. They write an excellent profile of themselves thinking this will attract "Mr. Right" but don't post their picture because they want the man to fall for "the real" them, not how they look. Big mistake. Get his attention with the visual first and then your wonderful personality, intelligence, professionalism, etc. later. Remember, you're not trying to attract another woman so you need to think like a man and what stimulates him. You don't try to catch a fish with a slice of onion; you use a worm.

Think men are just superficial jerks? According to John Townsend in his book "What Women Want-What Men Want," women law students were willing to date homely-looking men as long as they thought they were training to be doctors. Wow! What a bunch of gold diggers! They didn't care so much about a man's looks as long as he had the potential of making big bucks and being successful.

The same study showed that male law students were willing to date a female law student or school teacher as long as she **wasn't** homely-looking. A man doesn't initially care about a woman's potential for financial success as he feels that is his responsibility but since he is so visual, she can't look like a dog. Wow! How shallow can you be?

Who is worse; the men or the women? Neither. We are just different and that is ok.

We should appreciate what is important to each of us without criticism or judgement because we are not going to change nature. Once you understand and accept the differences, you can accomodate and appreciate your mate and you both will be happy. If you try to fight the differences by saying the other is "wrong," you will wind up miserable and frustrated.

30

"Stop The Constant Nagging"

"In the USA alone, there are more than 2000 cases a year of men murdering their wives and claiming that their nagging drove them to it."[28] I guess it can be dangerous to nag!

Women are frustrated with men because men don't do what they're told. You say: "When are you going to finally clean out that filthy garage so I can get my car back in it?" He says: "I'll get to it soon." Every Saturday you nag him to clean the garage but he doesn't do it. It's not that he's trying to give you a hard time; he's just not ready to do it. Let it go. He will get to it eventually. He has to work up to it.

Women think that nagging will change a man. It won't. He will just become resentful and belligerent. He will tune you out and not listen to anything you have to say because he thinks you're being a raving wacko. He doesn't see anything wrong in waiting for the right time to clean that garage. It's just not that important to him.

Pick your battles with a man. If you nag him about every little thing, he won't listen to you when it is something you really feel is important. You are not going to change him so just let it go and not obsess about it.

28 "Why Men Don't Have a Clue and Women Always Need More Shoes" by Barbara and Allan Pease. Broadway Books

A woman thinks that if her man doesn't clean the garage right away, he doesn't love her. Men are not that complicated; especially when it comes to love. They're simple (you know that already). They just don't want to do it right then and it has nothing to do with the woman or how they feel about her. They don't see the correlation.

Like denying their personalities change during a PMS tirade, women don't think they nag. "Women deny nagging because it is unconscious."[29] They may call it "positive reinforcement" or perhaps "gentle persuasion." They never think of themselves as naggers as that is too negative a connotation.

According to the book "Why Men Don't Have a Clue and Women Always Need More Shoes" by Barbara and Allan Pease, there are even 5 types of nagging (I thought nagging was just nagging). Single subject nagging, multi-nagging, beneficial nag, third-party nag, and advance nag. You know something is bad when they can come up with 5 types!

Women can even vary the tone of their voices to nag. They can say something like: "That shirt you bought yesterday really looks great on you." With the right condescending tone, it could mean: "That shirt you picked out looks hideous so I will go back with you and pick out a better one because you are too stupid to pick out a good shirt on your own." Women have many more voice tones than men and use them constantly to communicate their feelings without saying any nasty words. Listen to them talk to children. A man would just say to another man: "I see you picked that shirt out yourself. It looks like crap. Take your wife with you next time."

Ultimatums do not work with men. If you have been nagging a man to do something and then give him an ultimatum ("If you

[29] Excerpted from "Opposite Sides of the Bed" by Cris Evatt with permission of Red Wheel/Weiser abd Conari Press.

don't clean that garage, I will never make supper for you again because you're an inconsiderate bum."), he will stock up on tv dinners.

Men consider an ultimatum a challenge to their manhood. It's like challenging a caveman with a stick. It is no longer a simple disagreement. They can't back down now and will go to hell and back before they give in to an ultimatum. Is having that garage cleaned worth this kind of fight? Pick your battles wisely as they could be very costly to the relationship. Understand what escalates an argument into an all-out, potentially relationship-ending disaster for a man and tread carefully.

I learned some valuable lessons about guys when I was in sports. I remember a meet at Lycoming College in Williamsport, PA where I was a varsity swimmer. Coach Mort Rauff told me I had to swim an event I never swam before and wasn't very good doing. Just before I got up on the blocks to start the event, the guy next to me from another college swore at me. It was a direct confrontation that really got me angry and the adrenaline was flowing. I came in first for that event. If you confront a man and challenge him, he will do whatever is necessary to beat you. Don't confront a man unless you are ready for the consequences. Give him an out.

One of the reasons men don't respond well to nagging is that it reminds them of their mothers telling them what to do all the time. Men don't want to be treated like little boys and they don't need another mother. They are grown men and expect to be treated as such. Women think that men are immature kids (they sometimes act that way!) and what works for kids should work for these Neanderthal creatures they marry. Sure, men like their toys (cars, boats, tools, etc.) but because that's what challenges them. Nagging won't work over the long-haul. Men will resent the constant criticism and eventually rebel.

Never say: "I told you so."

"My wife never let anything go. All she did was bitch, bitch, bitch." If your man did something wrong or stupid 20 years ago, let it go! Women cannot let things go and will bring up a man's failures over and over again to beat him into the ground. Men don't mind taking a hit for a mistake but won't tolerate being chastised forever. If you continue to berate him for past mistakes rather than looking ahead to pleasant times, you will destroy the relationship.

Understand that nagging doesn't work over the long-haul. Compliment him when he eventually cleans the garage and forget that it took him 6 months to get around to it. Let the small things slide and you will have a more satisfying relationship.

"Why Ask For Directions? I'm Not Lost"

The standard joke about men is that they refuse to ask for directions and it is true! Women don't understand why men refuse to ask for directions and will say: "Why don't you just stop and ask somebody how to get there?"

It is important to understand why men don't ask for help in order to have a better relationship with a man. It will reduce your frustration and anxiety.

Men won't ask for directions when driving even when it is obvious they are lost.

I'm pathetic in a store. You can recognize me by the guy wandering around for an hour looking for something rather than asking a clerk. It just doesn't seem to make sense.

And a man will try to put a bike together without reading the directions because every real man should know how to put a bike together! Only wimps ask for directions.

I asked men why they absolutely refuse to ask for any kind of directions.

"Because we're not lost; we're just exploring."

"Because you look like an idiot."

"It's not macho."

"They don't want to look bad in front of their ladies."

"The only reason to ask for directions is to keep her from pestering me."

"We already know how to get there."

"We don't like being wrong."

"I'm too independent to ask for directions."

"Who's in a hurry?"

"I wouldn't ask a woman because I know she won't have the correct answer."

"As long as I have a tank of gas, I know where I'm going."

"We are hunters. We don't need no stinking map. It's all in our heads."

"Real men don't get lost."

"We're not lost. We're just disoriented."

"Men are hardwired to do things independently."

"Men don't want to admit they need something or need help."

"Hey, I just asked for directions two weeks ago!"

"Men can read maps so why ask for directions?"

"It's more fun to search on your own."

"You look like an idiot if you ask for directions."

"It's humiliating."

So there you have it. All the reasons men hate to ask for directions. None of them make sense.

Never tell a man he should ask for directions or get help of any kind. It is an insult to his manliness and he will be offended. Let him drive on for a while without saying anything. If it takes him an extra hour to put something together because he didn't read the directions, so be it. Don't say anything!

It is important to understand this quirk in a man's nature so you don't have to agonize over it.

Actually, it's pretty amusing and harmless. Men are just men and asking for help is a sign of weakness and no man wants to appear weak. Appreciate that he needs to be strong and that is why he doesn't ask for directions. He wants to be your hero so just let him stay lost for a while!

32

The Ideal Middle-Aged Woman

The ideal middle-aged woman should be a poor parallel parker and a poor map reader. According to the book "Why Men Don't Listen and Women Can't Read Maps" by Barbara and Allan Pease, very feminine women can't parallel park or read maps because they are low on testosterone. Men are better because they have high testosterone which improves spatial ability. I guess if you are a good parallel parker and map reader, you are out of luck with men!

We all know there is no "ideal" middle-aged woman because everyone (even men) have their faults. But there are certain common traits men are looking for in a woman which women will find informative and amusing.

Men responded to my survey about the qualities of the ideal middle-aged woman:

"Friendly and intelligent above everything else."

"Outgoing, independent, communicative, positive, empathetic as well as nurturing."

"Good sense of humor, adventurous, spontaneous."

"She is as good listening as she is talking."

"Sexy, smart, wants physical activity beyond the bedroom."

"A hooker in the bedroom but classy and sweet in public."

"Supportive without nagging."

"She will be my best friend, appreciates my sense of humor, and puts up with me."

"She enjoys life and her relationship with me."

"Likes to be social but knows when to go home."

"Easy going, patient, and a great sense of humor."

"Independent but bendable."

"She has a positive look on life."

"Doesn't nag."

"Smart, caring, and has a sense of humor."

"Quiet, almost shy nature."

"Happy, sexy, doesn't nag, and takes care of me."

"Well-read but not too outspoken in public."

"Respectful."

"Blind to my obvious flaws and forgiving without being asked."

"Laughs at herself, me, and life."

Middle-aged men want a woman, not a woman trying to be a man. She should be feminine. She should look and act feminine. She should be direct and assertive without being aggressive or over-bearing.

As you can see by the responses of men, sex is not the top priority for men when seeking their "ideal" woman. That's probably a surprise to women who think men only want "one thing."

She should be easy to understand and open with her thoughts. If she makes everything too complicated, he will give up. Remember that men are very simple creatures and they need simple in return.

Above all, the ideal woman is positive, upbeat, smiles, and shows that she wants to be with her man by supporting him. She keeps criticism to a minimum. Attitude and personality are everything.

Laugh with your man every day. Laugh at yourself once-in-a-while too!

Make more good memories than bad.

A great body can't make up for a miserable personality. Be nice. Loosen up!

Men would love to go to bed and have wild sex with a dumb bimbo actress type but don't want to marry her. Don't be jealous of the bimbos; they don't have any real relationships with men. Men in their lives are just using them. Men want women who are intelligent and thoughtful. He wants someone he can be proud of. Someone other men will admire and want but can't have.

She also has to be a good kisser. Who likes a poor kisser? Not sloppy or too aggressive. Warm, moist, slow, and sensual kisses are the best. He should feel as if he is making love kissing you. A kiss is the gateway to passion and must be a romantic haven for him. Make every kiss special and he will long for more and give you more in return.

Be spontaneous. Men love spontaneity; especially sexually. Always be a little challenging for him so he has to pursue you.

Men want to do things outdoors with their mates. It came up repeatedly in my survey along with the word adventurous so don't forget those two things: outdoor activities and adventurous.

Find a nice outdoor activity you **both** like. It could be gardening, bike riding, hiking in the woods, or bungy jumping. Be open to new adventures with him because he always needs a challenge. Men hate boredom or boring mates.

Make an effort to do things with your man. Take a shower with him. Make him feel successful and encourage him to greater things. Leave sweet notes for him. Touch him. Make time for him where the two of you are alone. Plan a vacation for just the two of you where both of you want to go. Be creative and above all, be happy!

So what does the "ideal" middle-aged woman look like? I asked men throughout the United States that question.

There were no if's, and's, or butt's; **men don't like women with big butts**. Most men prefer women with medium sized butts. Some like small butts. But no one said they like huge butts.

Men don't like fat unless it is on the chest area. **"She has to have weight proportionate to the other parts of her body."**

Men don't like skinny either. **"She has to have some meat on her bones."** Men would prefer a woman to be a "little" overweight than skinny. **" I don't want a woman who is too Rubenesque."**

One man stated that once a woman has you hooked, she gains 30 pounds. I discuss this "deception" men feel in other parts of this book. Men don't like to be deceived and it will be reflected in their actions later in the relationship. Men are very simple and don't like change unless they initiate it.

Another man said he doesn't like the "Barbie Doll image." Take that for what you wish. I guess he doesn't like the fake look.

"She should be shaved clean." I didn't expect that answer but as a gentleman, assume she should have no facial hair...

How tall should this "ideal woman" be? About 5'7" seems to be the consensus. **"I don't want her taller than me."** Men don't like to be with a woman who is taller than he. It's probably that macho thing.

Hair color mentioned the most was **red**. Second was brown and a distant third was blonde. No gray hair ladies! So much for blondes having more fun.

One man said: **"Dark red or blue hair, large breast, and nice, tight rear."** I guess if you have blue hair, one breast, and a tight ass you are all set with this guy.

Her hair should be long. Shoulder length "or longer" was preferred the most. I know, middle-aged women say long hair on older women looks silly and out-dated, doesn't have the luster it used to have, etc. Maybe to you, but to men, it is attractive and sexy even on middle-aged women. Why do you think men go after those young teeny-boppers? I know, short hair is easier to take care of. We have heard all the excuses. Do you want to be attractive to a man or not? Long hair is what men want.

What about breasts? As you would imagine, most men want a woman with big breasts. It must be that primal mating thing that attracts men to women with big breasts ideal for nursing. However, men wanted natural breasts, not ones enhanced by cosmetic surgery. It seems they are more attracted to smaller breasts if they are natural compared to large, unnatural breasts. There is a different, harder feel to some enhanced breasts that men don't find appealing. They also want a woman with nice nipples.

What do men think about cosmetic surgery to enhance a woman's appearance? As I said in the previous paragraph, they don't like breast enhancements. In general, men did not like cosmetic surgery at all. That surprised me as I thought women went through cosmetic surgery to attract and please men. It doesn't seem necessary and can actually be a detractor.

"I think that God made a person the way they are and they shouldn't change that."

"No. After the surgery, she constantly wanted me to say how much I liked them."

"I personally don't think it's necessary unless it's for reconstructive situations."

"No. Be satisfied and use what they have."

"Sure. If it makes them feel better about themselves."

"It's ok if she's paying for it because I won't be breaking in those implants!"

"Personality is more important."

"No. After surgery, those scars are not pretty."

Shave your legs and underarms so you are soft and inviting. Bad breath, yellow teeth, a moustache larger than his, and chicken-flab of any kind are real turn-offs to a man.

Too much makeup leads him to believe you have something to hide or are trashy. Keep it light.

Make sure your bra fits and enhances your attributes rather than boobs gushing out the sides like jelly squeezed from a doughnut.

Don't look cheap. You can look like a million bucks without spending a million. Spend time taking care of your looks. Men are visual so it is important.

Sexy underwear is a must. Anything baggy reminds him of his grandmother or aunt. Get rid of anything flannel.

Dress and act a little sexy (not too sexy), act confident but not cocky, look like you are inviting him to talk with you, and most important: **smile**. Men look to a woman for comfort, reassurance, and joy.

What is the first thing you notice about a woman when you meet that attracts you to her? That was one of the questions I posed to middle-aged men. One main said: **"I like a woman that does her nails and does her toenails with polish."** He obviously has some problems! Most men said: **"Her body, particularly her breasts. I know, I am shallow!"**

The close second was a woman's eyes and then her smile.

A woman who dresses well emphasizing her breasts and eyes along with a pleasant demeanor and smile will instantly attract men. **"Her happy glow attracts me."**

So there you have it! The personality and looks of the "ideal" woman. Be that "ideal" woman to him and you will have him for life!

33

What Men Want To Tell Women In America Today

I asked middle-aged men throughout America what they would like to tell women if they had the opportunity and some of their responses were enlightening. See what you think!

"Loosen up. Don't take life or yourself so seriously."

"Don't play stupid games."

"Be a woman, not a Gloria Steinhem."

"Be yourself. Don't try to be one of the guys."

"Don't think men are only out for a good time."

"You would be surprised what a little give and take can do for you."

"Don't blame us. We were made in God's image."

"Quit bitchin about every little thing."

"Don't regurgitate the past. We forgot it a long time ago."

"We long for the return of the traditional family and wish women did so too."

"If you see something you want, ask for it. Don't wait for it to hit you in the butt!"

"Don't look like a bum in public."

"Be more adventurous. Try new things."

"Realize that your man's needs change over time and a large part of love is need-fulfillment."

"I'd like to be a woman for a day because I know they have the power of the species."

"Stick with it. I'm out there"

"Stop running men down in public."

"Be conservative in the streets and wild in the sheets."

"Just once a week let me know that you appreciate me and what I do for you."

"Treat me with respect and you will get it in return."

"Walk beside me. Not in front or behind."

"Spread your freakin legs once-in-a-while!"

"Lighten up!"

"Don't analyze the crap out of everything."

"Too many of you have personalities of she-bears."

"Since you now consider yourselves equals to men, stop looking to men for your security!"

"Drop the attitude!"

"Find a way to respect your man and build him up rather than tear him down."

"Listen to us once-in-a-while."

"Help him to be faithful."

"Don't change after you have us."

"Be patient with us. We take more time to learn your feelings."

Many men said they want to tell women to just lighten up. They think women have become too serious and just aren't fun anymore. They want to be with upbeat women who make them feel good.

Of course, men think they are sex-starved and need more sex so that was a common theme not to be ignored. You should be a good sexual match.

We have covered most of the above topics in previous chapters so you should be aware of their importance to men. They are trying to communicate their needs and desires with you!

34

What Middle-Aged Men Want From Women

You already know from reading this book all of the things middle-aged men want from women!

Here are some more answers from middle-aged men:

"Respect, great sex, and support for my dreams and ambitions."

"Companionship, a maid, a workout partner, and respect."

"Sex is a must but a life-long, true, devoted woman too."

"Companionship, good sex, good cooking, don't nag, take care of her appearance, and don't look over my shoulder while I'm doing this survey!"

"Forgiveness and blindness to my obvious flaws."

"I want her to be my friend."

"Everything."

"Sex on a regular basis."

"A workout partner."

"Great companionship will bring the respect and the great sex."

"Affection and respect."

As you would expect, sex is what men want the most from women. It is that natural sexual drive men have and how they communicate with their mate.

I was really interested to see what things, other than the obvious sex topic, men want from women as women say that is all men want from them. "All he wants is sex. Men are just sex maniacs! He should want me for me, not just my body."

The second most mentioned thing middle-aged men want from women is companionship. Today's men don't feel their mates are providing that to them and that is very sad. Men are lonely.

It used to be that you would be best friends first and lovers or a married couple thereafter. Not now. Men don't see the women in their lives as their best friends anymore. In fact, many men see women as their adversaries as they are constantly thrust into competing with them.

When surveyed, women said they would rather be on a desert island with Mel Gibson or their best girlfriend than their own husbands! On the other hand, men said they would want to be with their wives (not Pamela Anderson) on the island. What a disappointing commentary on relationships. Women would rather be with someone other than their own mates and men are starting to realize where they stand.

A good companion is someone you enjoy doing everyday

things with. Someone who enjoys the same things as you, supports you, and is fun to be with without constant confrontation or ridicule. Companions are best friends. Be his best friend.

The third most mentioned thing that men want from women is respect. I devoted a separate chapter to that topic as it is so important to a man and his happiness. If you don't respect your man, you can't love him and he won't love you back. Without respect, a man is nothing. He feels worthless and will never be happy. Cultivate that respect for him and he will respond in wonderful ways.

Every man has traits which you can respect and admire. Find those traits and tell him how much you respect him. After all, you picked him to be your mate, didn't you? There must have been things you respected in him when you first met.

If you satisfy your man's sexual needs, be his companion, respect him for the man he is and what he does for you, communicate with him in ways he understands, allow him little adventures and challenges, don't dwell on his mistakes, and maintain an upbeat and positive attitude, you will attract and keep the man of your dreams.

If his needs are being fulfilled, he will love you more deeply than you ever imagined and will also support your happiness. He really wants you to be happy!

You now know that men are very simple in their desires and also know how to find and keep "Mr. Right." You have all the tools to have a happy and satisfying relationship with your middle-aged man. Use those tools and start enjoying life with your man!

SURVEY FOR WOMEN

Share your opinions for C. Bruce Wells' next book
"What Middle-Aged **Women** Want From Men" by completing
the survey for women at: www.cbrucewells.com

NEED A SPEAKER?

Bruce would love to speak at your next event!
He is humorous and informative!

Call his office at: (315) 597-3544 or visit his website at:
www.cbrucewells.com

ISBN 1412050294